THE GREATEST INSTRUMENT
for Promoting Harmony and Civilization

Excerpts from the Bahá'í Writings
and Related Sources on the Question of
an International Auxiliary Language

edited and introduced by

Gregory P. Meyjes

George Ronald
Oxford

George Ronald, *Publisher*
Oxford
www.grbooks.com

*A catalogue record for this book is available
from the British Library*

ISBN 978-0-85398-591-4

Cover design: Steiner Graphics

O members of parliaments throughout the world! Select ye a single language for the use of all on earth, and adopt ye likewise a common script . . . This will be the cause of unity, could ye but comprehend it, and the greatest instrument for promoting harmony and civilization, would that ye might understand!¹

Bahá'u'lláh

Contents

Acknowledgements

It gives one pause to realize that this unique collection of Bahá'í writings results from collaboration and reinvention that spans multiple decades, countries and continents. Consequently, the editor feels unequal to the charge of paying just tribute to the efforts of all parties concerned. This 'group' venture, loosely arranged across time and place, is manifestly indebted to the dedication and resolve of all contributing parties, known or unknown.

It is incontestable, however, that the project crucially depended on the initiative and tireless efforts of two consecutive secretaries of the Frankfurt-based Bahá'í Esperanto League (BEL), John T. Dale Jr. and Bernhard Westerhoff. To promote BEL and its agenda, they initially compiled the bulk of the material, with generous and vital archival assistance from the Research Department of the Bahá'í World Centre as well as with wise and patient guidance from Ulrich Gollmer, long-time editor at Bahá'í-Verlag Deutschland.

Most of the groundwork thus essentially laid, the present editor took over the project with the stated vision of completing the volume while transforming it into one that presented Bahá'í teachings on the international auxiliary language without bias towards any particular language and for all readers regardless of their ideological, religious or academic background. In the spirit of inclusion, neutrality and accessibility – and with valued graduate research assistance of Marcia Bost – the manuscript was thus reorganized, partly retranslated, revised, edited and extended.

Ultimately, through edifying collaboration with the publisher's Wendi Momen, the volume attained its present form. It will, it is hoped, attract a broad variety of readers from throughout the world community. May it inspire and instruct those who study and reflect on it, everywhere.

Publisher's Note

This book brings together a number of passages from both written and oral sources about the Bahá'í teaching regarding an international auxiliary language. We have tried to remain faithful to the original English-language texts by retaining the original spellings and orthographic and/or punctuation inconsistencies, including, for example, Baha'o'llah for Bahá'u'lláh, and alternative spellings, for example, Syrili for Cyrillic. Minor corrections have been made to punctuation for clarity, particularly in passages in chapter VI. British spelling has been used for consistency throughout.

'Abdu'l-Bahá while on His travels in the West between 1911 and 1913 gave a large number of formal and informal talks and interviews. In many instances the only record we have of these are the notes taken by those present, so-called 'pilgrims' notes', by various authors. As we cannot be sure that these notes are completely accurate, in the present volume we have indicated these by the phrase 'attributed to 'Abdu'l-Bahá'. Such passages are to be used with caution, as their reliability or authenticity cannot be conclusively established. They are not to be considered as authoritative writings of the Bahá'í Faith.

The day is approaching when all the peoples of the world
will have adopted one universal language and one common script.
When this is achieved, to whatsoever city a man may journey,
it shall be as if he were entering his own home.
These things are obligatory and absolutely essential.
It is incumbent upon every man of insight and understanding
to strive to translate that which hath been written into reality and action.[2]
Bahá'u'lláh

Introduction

We inhabit a world of paradox. While global networks strengthen, so do local initiatives. As cultural distances shorten, cultural differences are more keenly felt. While inter-civilizational frictions may mount, our interconnectedness grows more irrefutable each day. Such are the perplexing contradictions of our times – affecting us all, irrespective of our social, cultural or philosophical vantage point.

Since global communication concerns us all, this volume is addressed to readers from all walks of life, regardless of religious or professional background. Its principal purpose is to inform and inspire. Explanations – whether factual, terminological, historical, doctrinal or conceptual – are kept to a minimum. They serve first and foremost to aid comprehension. Whether we come to the text as communication specialists or linguists,

Esperantists or translators, monolinguals or polyglots, Buddhists or agnostics, politicians or community advocates, educators, students or concerned citizens, this unique collection of quotations from the Bahá'í writings on the question of an international auxiliary language, in part unavailable in print elsewhere, is potentially of interest to all.

The Bahá'í principle of an International Auxiliary Language (IAL) represents a novel paradigm for the establishment of peaceful and reciprocal relations among the world's ethno-linguistic traditions, a wide-ranging blueprint for a world in which language diversity is more equitably practised even while cultural exchange is more systemically established.

As a cornerstone of global concord, the IAL principle is aimed at preventing and resolving destructive tensions between the world's myriad native traditions – and to offer a solid and sustainable platform for fruitful interchange between them. That so noble a language policy vision should be religious in origin should not surprise those familiar with the history of auxiliary languages, whose protagonists were often both ideologically and practically motivated. The Bahá'í IAL doctrine lays claims to originate in a divine revelation poised to transform the inner and outer condition of humankind. In Bahá'í perspective, then, the IAL question, however utilitarian in appearance, is ethical in essence and divine in purpose – encompassing both outer and intangible conditions for establishing just, harmonious and synergistic relations between the peoples of the world.

It is to so remarkable a socio-linguistic doctrine that this unique collection of excerpts from the Bahá'í scriptures is dedicated. The Bahá'í canon, it should be said,

consists first and foremost of the Word revealed by
Bahá'u'lláh (1817–92), founder of the Bahá'í Faith, and by
His precursor, known as the Báb (1819–50). Their writings
are complemented by the words and writ of 'Abdu'l-Bahá
(1844–1921), appointed Interpreter of Bahá'u'lláh's pen,
and by clarifications on the part of both Shoghi Effendi
(1897–1957), appointed Guardian of the Faith, and the
Universal House of Justice, the highest Bahá'í governing
body, first elected in 1963. The sections of this volume
reflect this chronological and epistemological order.
Consequently, chapter I comprises seminal quotations of
Bahá'u'lláh. It is followed in chapter II by excerpts from
the writings of 'Abdu'l-Bahá and in chapter III by excerpts
from 'Abdu'l-Bahá's talks, which include addresses to
audiences in various European cities. Considerable space
is allotted to expositions of Shoghi Effendi in chapter IV
and the Universal House of Justice in chapter V. Passages
from other documents, including personal accounts, are
collected in chapter VI. Apart from those in chapter VI,
the selections in this publication are 'authenticated', in
that they have been officially attributed to their respective
authors by Bahá'í institutions. The Appendix contains
writings, largely from the above sources, on a number of
tangentially related language questions.

THE INTERNATIONAL AUXILIARY LANGUAGE PRINCIPLE

Rather than seeing global communication primarily in a mere functional light, the Bahá'í approach
is fundamentally spiritual in nature. It holds that
divine messengers renew social teachings from age
to age. It holds that each of these 'Manifestations of
God' initiates and inspires a new social order while

completing the previous dispensation – thus allowing humankind to 'carry forward an ever-advancing civilization,'[3] as Bahá'u'lláh asserts. The principle of the oneness of humanity, the 'pivot round which all the teachings of Bahá'u'lláh revolve,'[4] is regarded as the true source of the globally unifying processes at work today, rooted as they are in a new divine age and revelation. Bahá'í scriptures, moreover, clarify that the unity of humankind is based on its equality with regard to diversities of language, religion and race and ethnicity. Both unity and equality reflect divine purpose and neither is attainable without the other. Bahá'í writ thus foretells a world at once unified and diverse, enhanced and informed by its manifold traditions, supported by cultural rights.[5]

Featuring prominently in Bahá'í guidance for achieving such unity through equality is the doctrine of the IAL, the inevitable adoption of which Bahá'u'lláh portrays as a key sign of the 'coming of age' of humankind.[6] Whether especially created, or chosen from among existing or extinct natural languages, IAL is to enable unfettered interchange between native speech communities, the primary importance of which is undisputed. IAL, then, is meant to serve the twin goals of fostering international unity and cultural equity by facilitating unencumbered intercultural exchange even as it protects native language traditions from undue outward pressures. The 'establishment of order in the world and the tranquillity of the nations' depend on justice, Bahá'u'lláh proclaims.[7] IAL addresses the world's need for 'cultural justice' (Meyjes, 1999) while promoting robust communication among native-language communities worldwide. The Universal House of Justice further elucidates that IAL should be chosen by the 'governments of the world through their parliaments,'[8] thus implying a more formal introduction than that of any lingua franca present or past, including English. On the other hand, its status as auxiliary points to its secondary standing *vis-à-vis* primary language traditions, which retain their preeminent role of informing primary speech communities for the foreseeable future. IAL's standing as ancillary to mother tongues is reflected in the provision that IAL be taught in schools rather than be acquired at home. That IAL will not impede the development of the native-language acquisition process is reflected in the provision that 'in the schools of the future two languages will be taught – the mother tongue and this international auxiliary tongue.'[9] Indeed, Bahá'í scriptural allusions to the desired learnability of IAL further corroborate its non-primary position, since the question of IAL learnability is inherently secondary to mother-tongue acquisition. Moreover, absent from Bahá'í writ is the notion of an Adamic or otherwise intrinsically superior divine language[10] or of a particular language to be selected because of its geo-political or socially dominant role – though it is specified that IAL be fit for unlimited international communication and that it include a writing system. In essence, the Bahá'í doctrine of IAL calls for

a) the selection by expert representatives of governments,
b) of a natural or constructed, living or classical, functionally adequate human language,
c) and script,
d) for free and effective communication among native speakers of the world's diverse language communities,

e) to be taught as secondary to native languages world-wide,

f) thus favouring the language rights of primary speech communities,

g) as required for a more profoundly harmonious world community, and

h) the further development of its unity.[11]

HISTORICAL PERSPECTIVE

Of the two periods in history marked by heightened preoccupation with IALs, the first occurred in 17th-century Europe. Torn between a return to a Renaissance use of classical Latin for scientific discourse, the emergence of vernacular languages brought on by national awareness, Protestantism and the influence of the printing press technology, scientists developed an increased interest in objective analysis of the universe.[12] Operating within Christian societies, they were frequently swayed by prevailing interpretations of Genesis 2:19,[13] which held that the language of Adam reflected reality most perfectly, its 'naturalness' corrupted by other tongues as they developed through time, via the Babel phenomenon. None of the human languages, it was often felt, offered unequivocal access to 'real knowledge'. Calling for a medium to express the universe within and beyond man independently of the constraints of convention, culture and context, they sought to create a 'universal language' or 'real character' with which to capture existence more perfectly. Encouraged by novel insights into algebra, shorthand, cryptograms and ideograms, they searched for a more regular, real and ultimately simpler code than that of traditional natural languages.

With the confidence of the Enlightenment, distinguished thinkers such as John Locke, Marin Mersenne
and Sir Isaac Newton viewed these efforts as beneficial
to science and humanity. In hopes of representing the
universe objectively, some set out to construct 'philosophical' languages based on logical concepts and
principles; focusing instead on existing lexical items,
others strove to create 'universal languages' based on
super-vocabularies. The more rationalistically inclined,
such as Gottfried Leibniz and René Descartes, focused
on universal concepts while the more empirically
minded, like Francis Bacon and David Hume, tried to
classify observables. All were concerned with science in
service of society. John Comenius's 'pansophic' language
project, for instance, was intended both to articulate all
knowledge and to bring together a humanity estranged
through the curse of Babel. In the end, even such
prominent philosophical language schemes as George
Dalgarno's *Ars Signorum* (*The Art of Signs*, 1661) and
John Wilkins's 'Essay Towards a Real Character and
a Philosophical Language' (1668) suffered from fatal
logical and practical drawbacks. Parallels between these
efforts and later auxiliary language schemes are limited,
however, since the latter tended neither to reject natural
language on logical grounds nor claim to catalogue all –
much less ontologically 'real' – knowledge, in an ideal
sense.

In the wake of Bahá'u'lláh's declaration in 1863, the late
19th and early 20th centuries witnessed a renewed surge
of interest in auxiliary languages. Advocates saw linguistic diversity as a burden to international understanding
in an interdependent world – a notion indirectly confirmed by Bahá'u'lláh's admonition 'that men's lives

may not be dissipated and wasted in learning divers languages'.[14] With support from well-known language specialists such as Louis Couturat,[15] Otto Jespersen,[16] Edward Sapir,[17] Johann Schleyer,[18] and later Mario Pei,[19] the idea spread to lay circles. A wide variety of languages was proposed, created or modified. With the exception of mixed systems such as Volapük ('world language'), this second generation of language projects was based on natural language and devoid of aprioristic notions of reality – though they remained influenced by the standards of simplicity and regularity of the earlier schemes. They included a) classical languages such as Latin; b) *Latino Sine Flexione* and other simplified classical languages; c) living languages like Spanish; d) English with regularized orthography and similarly simplified living languages, e) Basic English, *Français Fondamental* and the like, with drastically reduced vocabularies; f) *Welt-Deutsch* (*Wede*) or languages similarly restructured beyond their lexicon; g) naturalistic constructions akin to Novial, comprised of minimally altered elements taken from multiple tongues, h) autonomous creations from various grammars and vocabularies, structured as regularly as possible or desirable – such as Esperanto or Ido; and i) integrated constructed-language designs akin to Neo, made up of elements from Esperanto, Ido and Novial.

With its dozens of periodicals and hundreds of clubs and textbooks worldwide, the Volapük movement's dramatic rise in the late 19th century was initially considered irreversible. Its creator, a German priest and philologist named Johann Schleyer, both religiously inspired and linguistically renowned, had achieved a categorical improvement over the cumbersome

17th-century schemes. Despite the linguistic short-comings that precipitated its social demise, Schleyer's proposal is recognized as the *de facto* starting point of modern constructed languages, or 'conlangs'.

In large part, Esperanto's eventual ascent to *primus inter pares* is due to its originator's humility and political astuteness. To avoid the fate of Volapük, Ludwig Zamenhof, a Jewish oculist from Poland, invited others to propose enhancements to his brainchild,[20] thus facilitating its social and linguistic expansion – and reflecting the observation attributed to 'Abdu'l-Bahá that 'no one person can construct a Universal Language'.[21] Zamenhof's concern for the adoptability of the language fuelled his adaptability, which in turn stemmed from a desire to serve humanity. Not permitting his world view – called *Homaranismo* after *homarano*, or member of the human race – to thwart collaboration with more practically-minded Esperantists, he set the movement on a flexible trajectory past countless challenges that included multiple secessions, such as the derivation of Ido by a group of leading scientists. Though less visible than during their pre-World War I and interbellum heyday, Esperantists today make up some 95 per cent of all active 'interlinguists', with hundreds of thousands of engaged members in over one hundred countries. Some of them are Bahá'ís. Zamenhof's daughter Lidia, for instance, was an internationally active Esperantist and Bahá'í.[22] Bahá'ís and their institutions remain favourably disposed to the Esperanto movement today, aided by its geographical spread and encouraged as they are by 'Abdu'l-Bahá, Shoghi Effendi and the Universal House of Justice. That they have nonetheless stopped short of learning the language in large numbers is perhaps partly due to the Bahá'í IAL principle itself, which calls for a policy act rather than a popular movement, a *de jure* intergovernmental resolution rather than the mere pursuit of a social *fait accompli*. As the Bahá'í writings are entirely and explicitly open as to which language will be selected as the IAL, all natural or constructed languages are potential candidates and the ultimate selection is left entirely in the hands of future decision-makers. While Bahá'ís unreservedly support the concept of IAL and earnestly strive to bring it about, including through association with Esperantists and like-minded others, they have not *en masse* chosen the Esperanto language as the means to do so – confident that, as Abdu'l-Bahá reportedly states, the 'love and effort put into Esperanto will not be lost'.[23]

SOME ISSUES ARISING[24]

In testimony to human ingenuity, today countless languages continue to be constructed and their minutiae debated, including, for instance, among electronic gamers.[25] At issue are often age-old assumptions about simplicity, naturalness or regularity. Simplicity, for instance, is seen either in logical-cognitive terms or based on the innate grammatical properties of human language.[26] Yet the overriding concern tends to be learnability by adults and others past the increasingly questioned 'critical period' for innate language acquisition.[27] Whereas the Bahá'í concept of IAL is sympathetic to the choice of a language that is relatively easy to learn, its primary target is less likely to be the first cohort of adult learners immediately following its adoption but rather the subsequent generations of children who would learn it in school thereafter. Language-pedagogical factors could thus offset some of the structural considerations that have so long preoccupied proponents of artificial languages.

The cultural neutrality of the vocabularies of planned languages has also been of abiding concern to interlinguists – existing constructions, including Esperanto, being predominantly Eurocentric in lexico-grammatical terms. Bahá'í sources speak of a constructed language 'made up of words from all the languages',[28] as opposed to one less universally designed. In principle, the vocabularies of constructed IAL contenders could be revised for greater inclusivity. However, Bahá'í scriptural openness to the choice of either a natural or a planned language suggests that the universality of the IAL lexicon may not, or not always, be of primary concern, since the words and idioms of any natural language chosen would likely reflect the relatively specific heritage of its native speech community.

However, the extrinsic properties of IAL candidates have also caused concern. English is the majority mother tongue in certain influential countries, the official language of over 70 nations, and the most widely taught foreign tongue in human history, exceeding even the group of languages commonly referred to as Chinese in total number of competent speakers.[29] Some consider global English to be socio-culturally neutral, while others associate it with unprecedented socio-cultural dominance. At issue is whether World English can function in a sufficiently auxiliary capacity or whether the extra-linguistic hegemony of its speech communities serves to place undue pressure on cultural pluralism worldwide, depriving the future international community of the benefits of ethno-linguistic diversity and undermining the aforementioned environment of intercultural justice and symbiosis. While Bahá'í writings pay tribute to the cultural rights enshrined in linguistic plurality, they favour neither cultural nostalgia as an end in itself nor the maintenance of language diversity on cognitive grounds. They focus on shielding primary cultures from external tyranny but not on maintaining languages devoid of cultural significance, nor on resisting ethno-linguistic change *per se*.

Cultural change is normal and natural and the Bahá'í IAL doctrine far from precludes it. On the contrary, for the distant future Bahá'í writings speak of the gradual emergence of a truly world-embracing society, the 'one organic commonwealth' described by Shoghi Effendi.[30] It will have been steadily informed by harmonious exchange among myriad primary cultures. Eventually it will have need of its own language, one that may or may not be related to the IAL. These developments are as yet entirely premature. For the projectable future, we are faced with the task of bringing about a world that harmoniously operationalizes the equality of ethno-cultural traditions. The twin challenges of today – the validation of diverse cultural legacies and the promotion of equitable intercultural exchange – are inseparable. For either to be accomplished, both must be satisfied. For the fulfilment of this elusive duality, the Bahá'í teachings on the auxiliary language provide invaluable guidance and inspiration, representing, as Bahá'u'lláh states, 'the greatest instrument for promoting harmony and civilization'.[31]

Gregory Paul Meyjes
Atlanta, Georgia, 2015

THE GREATEST INSTRUMENT
FOR PROMOTING HARMONY AND
CIVILIZATION

I Writings of Bahá'u'lláh

O members of parliaments throughout the world! Select ye a single language for the use of all on earth, and adopt ye likewise a common script. God, verily, maketh plain for you that which shall profit you and enable you to be independent of others. He, of a truth, is the Most Bountiful, the All-Knowing, the All-Informed. This will be the cause of unity, could ye but comprehend it, and the greatest instrument for promoting harmony and civilization, would that ye might understand! (*Kitáb-i-Aqdas*)[32]

~

The third Glad-Tidings concerneth the study of divers languages. This decree hath formerly streamed forth from the Pen of the Most High: It behoveth the sovereigns of the world – may God assist them – or the ministers of the earth to take counsel together and to adopt one of the existing languages or a new one to be taught to children in schools throughout the world, and likewise one script. Thus the whole earth will come to be regarded as one country. Well is it with him who hearkeneth unto His Call and observeth that whereunto he is bidden by God, the Lord of the Mighty Throne. (Glad-Tidings: *Bishárát*)[33]

~

We have formerly ordained that people should converse in two languages, yet efforts must be made to reduce them to one, likewise the scripts of the world, that men's lives may not be dissipated and wasted in learning divers languages. Thus the whole earth would come to be regarded as one city and one land. (Words of Paradise: *Kalimát-i-Firdawsíyyih*)[34]

⤳

Whilst in the Prison of 'Akká, We revealed in the Crimson Book that which is conducive to the advancement of mankind and to the reconstruction of the world. The utterances set forth therein by the Pen of the Lord of creation include the following which constitute the fundamental principles for the administration of the affairs of men: . . . Languages must be reduced to one common language to be taught in all the schools of the world. (Tablet of the World: *Lawḥ-i-Dunyá*)[35]

⤳

The sixth Ishráq is union and concord amongst the children of men. From the beginning of time the light of unity hath shed its divine radiance upon the world, and the greatest means for the promotion of that unity is for the peoples of the world to understand one another's writing and speech. In former Epistles We have enjoined upon the Trustees of the House of Justice either to choose one language from among those now existing or to adopt a new one, and in like manner to select a common script, both of which should be taught in all the schools of the world. Thus will the earth be regarded as one country and one home. (Splendours: *Ishráqát*)[36]

❧

Likewise He saith: Among the things which are conducive to unity and concord and will cause the whole earth to be regarded as one country is that the divers languages be reduced to one language and in like manner the scripts used in the world be confined to a single script. It is incumbent upon all nations to appoint some men of understanding and erudition to convene a gathering and through joint consultation choose one language from among the varied existing languages, or create a new one, to be taught to the children in all the schools of the world. (Tablet of Maqṣúd: *Lawḥ-i-Maqṣúd*)[37]

❧

The day is approaching when all the peoples of the world will have adopted one universal language and one common script. When this is achieved, to whatsoever city a man may journey, it shall be as if he were entering his own home. These things are obligatory and absolutely essential. It is incumbent upon every man of insight and understanding to strive to translate that which hath been written into reality and action. (Tablet of Maqṣúd: *Lawḥ-i-Maqṣúd*)[38]

❧

One day, while in Constantinople, Kamál Páshá visited this Wronged One. Our conversation turned upon topics profitable unto man. He said that he had learned several languages. In reply We observed: 'You have wasted your life. It beseemeth you and the other officials of the Government to convene a gathering and choose one of the divers languages, and likewise one of the existing scripts, or else to create a new language and a new script to be taught children in schools through-out the world. They would, in this way, be acquiring only two languages, one their own native tongue, the other the language in which all the people of the world would converse. Were men to take fast hold on that which hath been mentioned, the whole earth would come to be regarded as one country, and the people would be relieved and freed from the necessity of acquiring and teaching different languages.' When in Our presence, he acquiesced, and even evinced great joy and complete satisfaction. We then told him to lay this matter before the officials and ministers of the Government, in order that it might be put into effect throughout the different countries. However, although he often returned to see Us after this, he never again referred to this subject, although that which had been suggested is conducive to the concord and the unity of the peoples of the world.

We fain would hope that the Persian Government will adopt it and carry it out. At present, a new language and a new script have been devised. If thou desirest, We will communicate them to thee. Our purpose is that all men may cleave unto that which will reduce unnecessary labour and exertion, so that their days may be befit-tingly spent and ended. God, verily, is the Helper, the

Knower, the Ordainer, the Omniscient. (*Epistle to the Son of the Wolf*)[39]

꙳

We have revealed in the Kitáb-i-Aqdas: 'O members of parliaments throughout the world! Select ye a single language for the use of all on earth, and adopt ye likewise a common script. God, verily, maketh plain for you that which shall profit you and enable you to be independent of others. He, of a truth, is the Most Bountiful, the All-Knowing, the All-Informed.' This binding commandment hath been sent down from the realm of ancient glory for the peoples of the world and, in particular, for the members of the parliaments, inasmuch as the task of executing the laws, the ordinances and statutes that have been sent down in the Book, hath been delegated unto the men of the divine Houses of Justice, and this law is the greatest means for achieving unity, and the mightiest instrument for promoting the intercourse and mutual affection of the people in all lands.

It is observable that most nations, by reason of the diversity of languages spoken by the peoples of the world, are deprived of intercourse and association, and of benefiting each from the other's fund of learning and wisdom. For this reason, and as an evidence of Our surpassing bounty and munificence, all have been commanded to select, and speak, a single language, whether this be newly created, or amongst the existing languages of the earth. If this be followed, the whole earth will become even as a single city, since all will be acquainted with each other's tongue, and understand each other's true intention. This will be the cause of the advancement and exaltation of the world. Should anyone travel from his native land, into whatsoever city he entereth it shall be as if he were entering his own home. Cleave ye thereunto, O legislators and citizens!

Were anyone to reflect awhile, he would perceive that whatsoever hath been sent down from the heaven of divine will, is naught but purest bounty, whose virtue redoundeth to the benefit of all. Certain souls, however, so suck from the breast of heedlessness and ignorance, that they disregard that which is good, the excellence of which, whether from the standpoint of reason or of tradition, is both clear and manifest; through hearkening unto the idle contentions of heedless souls, they have grown oblivious of that divine wisdom which is the cause and means for the advancement of the world and the upliftment of its peoples. They, of a surety, are in manifest loss.

Each people discourseth in its own language, such as the Turks in Turkish, the Iranians in Persian, the Arabs in Arabic, and the peoples of Europe in their own divers tongues. These tongues are current amongst the different peoples, and specific unto each group. Now, another language hath been commanded for all the peoples of the world, that all may be familiar with each other's speech, and understand each other's purpose. This is the portal of love and amity, of harmony and unity, and this is the most great conveyor of meaning, the key that unlocketh the treasure of Him Who is the Ancient of Days.

How many a soul hath been seen to spend his whole time in the acquisition of various tongues! How truly regrettable that a man should devote his life, which is the dearest of all things in the world, to matters of this

8

kind! The object of these exertions in learning the divers languages is to be able to apprehend the purpose of the many nations, and become apprised of whatsoever they possess. Now, were such people to act in accordance with what hath been commanded, it would suffice everyone, and all would be spared the need for these interminable efforts.

That which is beloved before Our throne is that all should speak in Arabic, for it is the richest of all the languages. Were anyone to become acquainted with the wealth and vastness of this eloquent tongue, he would assuredly select it. The Persian tongue is passing sweet, and, in the present Dispensation, the Tongue of God hath spoken in both Arabic and Persian tongues; yet it doth not have the vastness of the Arabic. Nay, in comparison, all the languages of the earth are limited, and shall remain so.

What hath been said of Arabic is in the nature of a preference; howbeit Our intention is that the peoples of the earth should select a single tongue, and that everyone should speak it. This is that which God hath ruled, and this is that which shall be of benefit to the people, if only they could apprehend it. In like manner, they should select a single script, apart from those peculiar unto the different peoples, and everyone should occupy themselves in using it, in order that all scripts may be seen as one script, and all languages as a single language. This will cause the hearts and souls of the peoples of the world to become united. He, verily, informeth you of that wherein is your advantage; cleave ye thereunto. He, verily, is the Admonisher, the Counsellor, the Expounder, the Disposer, the Compassionate, the All-Knowing, the All-Wise. At length, all languages and scripts will culminate in one, and the different regions of the earth shall be considered even as a single region. 'Then shalt thou see in it no irregularity or distortion.' (*Nafaḥát-i-Quds*)[40]

II Writings of 'Abdu'l-Bahá

O honoured lady! In cycles gone by, though harmony was established, yet, owing to the absence of means, the unity of all mankind could not have been achieved. Continents remained widely divided, nay even among the peoples of one and the same continent association and interchange of thought were wellnigh impossible. Consequently intercourse, understanding and unity amongst all the peoples and kindreds of the earth were unattainable. In this day, however, means of communication have multiplied, and the five continents of the earth have virtually merged into one. And for everyone it is now easy to travel to any land, to associate and exchange views with its peoples, and to become familiar, through publications, with the conditions, the religious beliefs and the thoughts of all men. In like manner all the members of the human family, whether peoples or governments, cities or villages, have become increasingly interdependent. For none is self-sufficiency any longer possible, inasmuch as political ties unite all peoples and nations, and the bonds of trade and industry, of agriculture and education, are being strengthened every day. Hence the unity of all mankind can in this day be achieved. Verily this is none other but one of the wonders of this wondrous age, this glorious century. Of this past ages have been deprived, for this century – the century of light – hath been endowed with unique and unprecedented glory, power and illumination. Hence the miraculous unfolding of a fresh marvel every day. Eventually it will be seen how bright its candles will burn in the assemblage of man.

Behold how its light is now dawning upon the world's darkened horizon. The first candle is unity in the political realm, the early glimmerings of which can now be discerned. The second candle is unity of thought in world undertakings, the consummation of which will ere long be witnessed. The third candle is unity in freedom which will surely come to pass. The fourth candle is unity in religion which is the corner-stone of the foundation itself, and which, by the power of God, will be revealed in all its splendour. The fifth candle is the unity of nations – a unity which in this century will be securely established, causing all the peoples of the world to regard themselves as citizens of one common fatherland. The sixth candle is unity of races, making of all that dwell on earth peoples and kindreds of one race. The seventh candle is unity of language, i.e. the choice of a universal tongue in which all peoples will be instructed and converse. Each and every one of these will inevitably come to pass, inasmuch as the power of the Kingdom of God will aid and assist in their realization. (Letter to Mrs Jane Elizabeth Whyte)[41]

And among the teachings of Bahá'u'lláh is the origination of one language that may be spread universally among the people. This teaching was revealed from the pen of Bahá'u'lláh in order that this universal language may eliminate misunderstandings from among mankind. (Letter to the Executive Committee of the Central Organization for a Durable Peace)[42]

As to the Esperantists, associate with them. Whenever you find one with capacity, convey to him the fragrances of Life . . .

It is evident that the Esperantists are receptive and thou art familiar with and expert in their language. Communicate also with the Esperantists of Germany and other places . . . Grieve not over the apathy and coldness of the Hague meeting. Put thy trust in God. Our hope is that among the people the Esperanto language may hereafter have a powerful effect. Thou hast now sown the seed. Assuredly it will grow. Its growth dependeth upon God. (Letter to an individual)[43]

∽

But regarding the universal language: Ere long significant and scientific discussions concerning this matter will arise among the people of discernment and insight and it will produce the desired result. (Letter to an individual)[44]

∽

Thou hast written regarding the language of Esperanto. This language will be spread and universalized to a certain degree, but later on a language more complete than this, or the same language will undergo some changes and alterations and will be adopted and become universal. I hope that Dr. Zamenhof become assisted by the invisible confirmation and do a great service to the world of humanity. (Letter to an individual)[45]

∽

Praise be to God that the Sun of Reality has shone forth with the utmost brilliancy from the eastern horizon. The regions of the world are flooded with its glorious light. There are many rays to this Sun: . . . The thirteenth ray is the spread of an auxiliary world language. (Letter to *The Asiatic Quarterly Review*)[46]

∾

Concerning the Esperanto language: The friends have already written numerous letters that have been published throughout the world. It is my earnest hope that when the Esperantists realize to what extent this language hath been favourably recommended, they may be attracted to the Cause, may endeavour to translate some of the important Tablets of Bahá'u'lláh into Esperanto and publish them, may set their faces toward the Abhá Kingdom and beseech divine aid and assistance for this mighty enterprise. (Letter translated from the Persian)[47]

∾

The question of universal peace is one of the principles of the teachings of Baha'o'llah. These teachings have other principles that make them complete, such as: The oneness of humanity; the investigation of truth and reality and the abandonment of old superstitions; unity and religious amity; that religion must be the cause of concord; that all religions must conform with science and reason; that there must be no religious, racial or national prejudices; that there must be a oneness of language – that is, the adoption of a universal auxiliary language, so that every mind shall know two languages, one the national tongue and the other the universal language . . . (Letter to the Honorable William Sulzer)[48]

~

His Honor, Dr. Fareed – Upon him be Baha-el-Abha! O servant of the Holy Threshold! You have written in regard to Esperanto and your speech before the Congress. It was most appropriate and acceptable. If possible meet with Dr. Zamenhof and show him the Kitab-el-Aqdas (Book of Laws) and translate the verse which concerns the Universal Language and tell him: This clear verse, which was revealed forty-five years ago, will prove the cause of spreading your Universal Language in all the East. The Bahais shall consider the study of this language as an incumbent duty upon them, and it will be to them a religious duty. Therefore, men, women, and children, all will acquire it. (Letter to Dr Ameen Fareed)[49]

~

III Talks and Remarks by 'Abdu'l-Bahá[50]

Address in Paris, 1913

In order to facilitate complete understanding between all people, a universal auxiliary language will be adopted and in the schools of the future two languages will be taught – the mother tongue and this international auxiliary tongue which will be either one of the existing languages or a new language made up of words from all the languages – the matter is to be determined by a confederation met for the purpose which shall represent all tribes and nations. This international tongue will be used in the work of the parliament of man – a supreme tribunal of the world which will be permanently established in order to arbitrate international questions.[51]

Address to the Esperantists of Edinburgh

Every movement which promotes unity and harmony in the world is good, and everything which creates discord and discontent is bad. This is a century of illumination, surpassing all others in its many discoveries, its great inventions, and its vast and varied undertakings. But the greatest achievement of the age in conferring profit and pleasure on mankind is the creation of an auxiliary language for all. Oneness of language creates oneness of heart. Oneness of language engenders peace and harmony. It sweeps away all misunderstandings among peoples. It establishes harmony among the children of men. It gives to the human intellect a broader conception, a more commanding point of view.

Today the greatest need of humanity is to understand and to be understood. With the help of the International Language, every individual member of a community can learn of world happenings and become in touch with the ethical and scientific discoveries of the age. The auxiliary international language gives to us the key – the key of keys – which unlocks the secrets of the past. By its aid every nation henceforth will be able easily and without difficulty to work out its own scientific discoveries.

It is a well-known fact that the Oriental student coming to the west, in his efforts to acquaint himself with the discoveries and achievements of western civilization, must spend precious years of his life in acquiring the language of the land to which he comes before he can turn to the study of the special science in which he is interested. For example, let us suppose that a youth from India, Persia, Turkestan or Arabia comes to this country to study medicine. He must first struggle with the English language for four years, to the exclusion of all else, before he can even begin the study of medicine. Whereas, if the auxiliary international language were taught in all the schools during his childhood, he would learn the language in his own country, and afterwards, wherever he wished to go, he could easily pursue his specialty without loss of some of the best years of his life.

Today if one wishes to travel abroad, even though possessed of several languages, he is likely to be seriously handicapped because he does not know the particular language of some one people. I have studied oriental languages profoundly and know the Arabic better than the Arabians themselves. I have studied Turkish and Persian in my native land, besides other languages of the East, nevertheless, when I visited the West I had to take an interpreter with me quite as if I knew no language. Now if the International Language were generally spoken, that and the Persian language would be sufficient for me in every country of the world.

Only think how the International Language will facilitate intercommunication among all the nations of the earth. Half of our lives are consumed in acquiring a knowledge of languages, for in this enlightened age every man who hopes to travel in Asia and Africa and Europe must learn several languages in order that he may converse with their peoples. But no sooner does he acquire one language than another is needed. Thus one's whole life may be passed in acquiring those languages which are a hindrance to international communication. The International Language frees humanity from all these problems.

In a word, to understand and be understood, there must be an international medium. The teacher and the pupil must know each other's language, in order that the teacher may impart his knowledge and the pupil receive it. In all the world there is nothing more important than to be understood by your fellow-men, for upon this depends the progress of civilization itself. To acquire a knowledge of the arts and sciences one must know how to speak, to understand and at the same time to make himself understood, and this matter of understanding and being understood depends on language.

Once establish this auxiliary language, and all will be enabled to understand each other.

I recall an incident which occurred in Bagdad. There were two friends who knew not each other's language. One fell ill, the other visited him, but not being able to express his sympathy in words, resorted to gesture, as if to say, 'How do you feel?' with another sign the sick man replied, 'I shall soon be dead'; and his visitor, believing the gesture to indicate that he was getting better, said, 'God be praised!'

From such illustrations you will admit that the greatest thing in the world is to be able to make yourself understood by your friends and to understand them, and that there is no greater handicap in the world than not to be able to communicate your thoughts to others. But with an auxiliary language all these difficulties disappear.

Now, praise be to God, that language has been created – Esperanto. This is one of the special gifts of this luminous century, one of the most remarkable achievements of this great age.[52]

〜

His Holiness Baha'o'llah many years ago wrote a book called 'The Most Holy Book', one of the fundamental principles of which is the necessity of creating an International Language, and He explains the great good and advantage that will result from its use.

Now let us thank the Lord because the Esperanto language has been created. We have commanded all the Bahais in the Orient to study this language very carefully, and ere long it will spread all over the East. I pray you,

Esperantists and non-Esperantists, to work with zeal for the spread of this language, for it will hasten the coming of that day, that millennial day, foretold by prophets and seers, that day when, it is said, the wolf and the lamb shall drink from the same fountain, the lion and the deer shall feed in the same pasture. The meaning of this holy word is that hostile races, warring nations, differing religions, shall become united in the spirit of love.

I repeat, the most important thing in the world is the realization of an auxiliary international language. Oneness of language will transform mankind into one world, remove religious misunderstandings, and unite East and West in the spirit of brotherhood and love. Oneness of language will change this world from many families into one family. This auxiliary international language will gather the nations under one standard, as if the five continents of the world had become one, for then mutual interchange of thought will be possible for all. It will remove ignorance and superstition, since each child of whatever race or nation can pursue his studies in science and art, needing but two languages – his own and the International.[53] The world of matter will become the expression of the world of mind. Then discoveries will be revealed, inventions will multiply, the sciences advance by leaps and bounds, the scientific culture of the earth will develop along broader lines. Then the nations will be enabled to utilize the latest and best thought, because expressed in the International Language.

If the International Language becomes a factor of the future, all the Eastern peoples will be enabled to acquaint themselves with the sciences of the West, and in turn the Western nations will become familiar with the thoughts and ideas of the East, thereby improving the condition of both. In short, with the establishment of this International Language the world of mankind will become another world and extraordinary will be the progress.[54] It is our hope, then, that the language Esperanto will soon spread throughout the whole world, in order that all people may be able to live together in the spirit of friendship and love.[55]

❦

Address to the Esperantists of Paris[56]

Abdul Baha said: Human undertakings are divided into two kinds – universal and personal.

Those efforts which create general interest are universal; their results are likewise universal for humanity has become interdependent. The international laws of to-day are of vast importance, for as international politics bring nations nearer to one another – and thus promote a bond of oneness which acts as a magnet to attract the divine confirmations – the results and benefits are limitless. Therefore, let us say that every universal cause is divine and every personal matter is human or limited.

The universal light for this planet is from the sun and the special electric ray which to-night illumines this banquet hall appears through the invention of man. In like manner the activities which are trying to establish solidarity between the nations and infuse the spirit of universalism in the hearts of the children of men are like unto divine rays from the sun of reality and the brightest ray is the coming of the universal language.

Its achievement is the greatest virtue of the age for such an instrument will remove misunderstandings from amongst the peoples of the earth and will cement their hearts together. This medium will enable each individual member of the human family to be informed of the scientific accomplishments of all.

The basis of knowledge and the excellencies of endeavour in this world are to teach and to be taught. To acquire sciences, and to teach them in turn, depends upon language, and when the international auxiliary tongue becomes universal it is easily conceivable that the acquirement of knowledge and instruction will likewise become universal.

No doubt you are aware that in the past ages a common language shared by various nations created a spirit of solidarity amongst them. For instance, thirteen hundred years ago there were many divergent nationalities in the Orient. There were Copts in Egypt, Syrians in Syria, Assyrians and Babylonians in Bagdad and along the rivers of Mesopotamia. There existed among these peoples rank hatred; but as they were gradually brought nearer through common protection and common interests, the Arabic language grew to be the means of intercommunication and they became as one nation. They all speak Arabic to this day. In Syria, if you ask any one of them, he will say, 'I am an Arab', though he be a Greek, an Egyptian, Syrian or Jew.

We say 'this man is a German, the other an Italian, a Frenchman, an Englishman', etc. All belong to the great human family yet language is the barrier between them. The greatest working basis for bringing about unity and harmony amongst the nations is the teaching of a universal tongue. Writing on this subject fifty years ago, His Holiness BAHA'O'LLAH declared that complete union between the various nations of the world would remain an unrealized dream until an international language was established.

Misunderstandings keep people from mutual association and these misunderstandings will not be dispelled except through the medium of a common ground of communication. Every intelligent man will bear testimony to this.

The people of the Orient are not fully informed of the events in the west and the west cannot put itself into sympathetic touch with the east. Their thoughts are enclosed in a casket. The universal language will be the master key to open it. Western books will be translated into that language and the east will become informed of the contents; likewise eastern lore will become the property of the west. Thus also will those misunderstandings which exist between the different religions be dispersed. Religious prejudices play havoc among the peoples and bring about warfare and strife and it is impossible to remove them without a common medium.

I am an Oriental and on this account I am shut out from your thoughts and you likewise from mine. A mutual language will become the mightiest means toward universal progress, for it will cement the east and the west. It will make the world one home and become the divine impulse for human advancement. It will upraise the standard of oneness of the world of humanity and make the earth a universal commonwealth. It will create love between the children of men and good fellowship between the various creeds.

Praise be to God, that Dr. Zamenhof has constructed the Esperanto language. It has all the potential qualities of universal adoption. All of us must be grateful and thankful to him for his noble effort, for in this matter he has served his fellow-man well. He has done a service which will bestow divine benefits on all peoples. With untiring effort and self-sacrifice on the part of its devotees it holds a promise of universal acceptance.

Therefore every one of us must study this language and make every effort to spread it, so that each day it may receive a wider recognition, be accepted by all nations and governments of the world and become a part of the curriculum of all the public schools. I hope that the business of the future international conferences and congresses will be carried on in Esperanto.

In the coming ages, two languages will be taught in the schools, one the native tongue, the other an international auxiliary language. Consider today how difficult is human communication. One may study fifty languages and travel through a country and still be at a loss. I myself speak several Oriental languages, but know no western tongue. Had this universal language pervaded the globe, I should have studied it and you would have been directly informed of my thoughts and I of yours and a special friendship would have been established between us.

Please send some teachers to Persia so that they may teach Esperanto to the younger generation. I have written asking some of them to come here to study it.

May it be promulgated rapidly; then the world of humanity will find eternal peace; all the nations will associate with one another like mothers and sisters, fathers and brothers, and each individual member of the community will be fully informed of the thoughts of all.

I am extremely grateful to you and thank you for these lofty efforts, for you have gathered at this banquet in a selfless endeavour to further this great end. Your hope is to render a mighty service to the world of humanity and for this exalted aim I congratulate you from the depths of my heart.[57]

⌒

Address given at 4 Avenue de Camoëns, Paris

One of the great steps towards universal peace would be the establishment of a universal language. Bahá'u'lláh commands that the servants of humanity should meet together, and either choose a language which now exists, or form a new one. This was revealed in the Kitáb-i-Aqdas forty years ago. It is there pointed out that the question of the diversity of tongues is a very difficult one. There are more than eight hundred languages in the world, and no person could acquire them all.

The races of mankind are not isolated as in former days. Now, in order to be in close relationship with all countries, it is necessary to be able to speak their tongues.

A universal language would make intercourse possible with every nation. Thus it would be needful to know two languages only, the mother tongue and the universal speech. The latter would enable a man to communicate with any and every man in the world!

A third language would not be needed. To be able to talk with a member of any race and country without requiring an interpreter, how helpful and restful to all!

Esperanto has been drawn up with this end in view: it is a fine invention and a splendid piece of work, but it needs perfecting. Esperanto as it stands is very difficult for some people.

An international Congress should be formed, consisting of delegates from every nation in the world, Eastern as well as Western. This Congress should form a language that could be acquired by all, and every country would thereby reap great benefit.

Until such a language is in use, the world will continue to feel the vast need of this means of intercourse. Difference of speech is one of the most fruitful causes of dislike and distrust that exists between nations, which are kept apart by their inability to understand each other's language more than by any other reason.

If everybody could speak one language, how much more easy it would be to serve humanity!

Therefore appreciate 'Esperanto', for it is the beginning of the carrying out of one of the most important of the Laws of Bahá'u'lláh, and it must continue to be improved and perfected.[58]

~

Address to Esperantists in Stuttgart

In the Cause of God, there is nothing greater than to bring people together in oneness, for oneness and harmony among the people will always primarily lead to progress. When we consider humanity in this perspective, we find widely differing opinions about the sources of oneness.

Patriotism is one of the ways to bind people in greater communality. Yet patriotism is not sufficient to unite the whole of mankind. For we know from former times that many civil wars have erupted among the various peoples. Another kind of commonality is racial unity. Yet it, too, cannot achieve the solidarity of humanity, since we know from the past that discord exists within the races as well.

A particular kind of oneness occurs through unity of language. Its effect is more pervasive. Language has often been the means for uniting diverse races and nationalities. Especially in Oriental countries this has become clear. The Egyptians, for instance, were a nation to themselves; the Assyrians also founded a great empire, and a large part of the ancient world was based on the Chaldean civilization. One language eventually gained precedence over the others and united them all, such that the Chaldeans, the Assyrians and the Egyptians forgot their designations and became one. We call them Arabs today. Why? It is because the Arabic language became dominant among all these peoples. If today we ask an Egyptian his nationality, he will say, 'I am an Arab.' Likewise, the Chaldeans and Assyrians would call themselves Arabs. This proves to us that language has the capacity to unite peoples in a single bond.

Modern nations face many conflicts and frictions among themselves, the greater part of which stem from misunderstandings of language. From this comes the idea that all peoples should have a common language. It would be far more effective than patriotism or race consciousness. Therefore, Bahá'u'lláh, who appeared in the East, thus included the establishment of a single language among His teachings, so that this international auxiliary language would become the strongest means for tying the diverse nations together. Misunderstandings between peoples and races will thus be dispelled. There are so many languages, that even if we learned ten, we could always encounter peoples who understand none of them. Image that a German, who has learned the German language, goes to France, he will need to learn French; should he wish to go to England, French will be of no avail. If he is an intelligent person who understands all three languages but wants to travel to Italy, he must learn Italian. If a person were such a genius as to have mastered all the languages of the West, what would he do with them in the East? In short, if anyone were such a genius as to learn all the languages of the world, what good would it do him? The best solution is therefore to establish an auxiliary language that is accepted by all peoples.

Dr. Zamenhof has discovered such a language. Once this language has been introduced in all the schools of the world, this will certainly lead the peoples to the pinnacle of understanding. Then everyone will have only two languages to learn: one the native tongue, the other the auxiliary language of the entire world. As the auxiliary language spreads throughout the world, many misunderstandings will disappear, since misunderstandings, as mentioned, cause the greatest harm and since the reason for all these misunderstandings is the very absence of the language itself. Let us take a present example: though I stand here before you, how difficult it is to make myself understood, and it is completely impossible to share my innermost self. Were the international auxiliary language already established, I could speak to you without these two interpreters. This international auxiliary language will constitute the secure foundation for binding the peoples together. It will be of vast significance, even for uniting the religions. In the Orient, we have many Jews, Christians and Muslims. To date, there has never been war between the Christian Arabs and the Muslim Arabs, as they could make themselves mutually understood. They are able to exchange their thoughts. By contrast, there was always war between the Turks, Bulgarians and Greeks, for they could never agree on a common language. All these points irrefutably demonstrate that an international auxiliary language will unite humanity.

If I knew your language, I could discuss all subjects with you without difficulty. Since at present this international auxiliary language is not that widespread, I need two interpreters. How difficult that is! How lovely, how splendid it would be to understand each other in one language. Then East and West could unite and we would feel like one nation. Let us all strive for Esperanto to become more widely disseminated, so that a great comradeship may be created among the people.

Whatever profits all is divine in origin. The rays of the sun shine equally for all; therefore, they are divine. The benefits of rain reflect on all; therefore, they are divine. Heavenly blessings come to all; therefore, they are divine. Thus, every means to unite humanity is divine in origin.

We can say that the universal auxiliary language Esperanto is one of the blessings that emanate from God, because we see its effects. We are to labour and exert ourselves to make this language part of the curriculum in all schools. If I were able to express my thoughts in this language, there would be many more things I could tell you. This would unite us more easily. It is the absolute duty of each of us to lend a hand and promote the learning of the general auxiliary language, for it will become the means for raising the banner of world peace and brotherhood. Due to the two-fold interpretation, I am unable to say more.[59]

The love and effort put into Esperanto will not be lost . . . but no one person can construct a Universal Language. It must be made by a Council representing all countries, and must contain words from different languages. It will be governed by the simplest rules, and there will be no exceptions; neither will there be gender, nor extra and silent letters. Everything indicated will have but one name. In Arabic there are hundreds of names for the camel! In the schools of each nation the mother tongue will be taught, as well as the revised Universal Language.[60]

A Message to Esperantists given in Washington DC

Today the greatest need of the world of humanity is discontinuance of the existing misunderstandings among nations. This can be accomplished through the unity of language. Unless the unity of language is realized, the Most Great Peace and the oneness of the human world cannot be effectively organized and established because the function of language is to portray the mysteries and secrets of human hearts. The heart is like a box, and language is the key. Only by using the key can we open the box and observe the gems it contains. Therefore, the question of an auxiliary international tongue has the utmost importance. Through this means international education and training become possible; the evidence and history of the past can be acquired. The spread of the known facts of the human world depends upon language. The explanation of divine teachings can only be through this medium. As long as diversity of tongues and lack of comprehension of other languages continue, these glorious aims cannot be realized. Therefore, the very first service to the world of man is to establish this auxiliary international means of communication. It will become the cause of the tranquillity of the human commonwealth. Through it sciences and arts will be spread among the nations, and it will prove to be the means of the progress and development of all races. We must endeavour with all our powers to establish this international auxiliary language throughout the world. It is my hope that it may be perfected through the bounties of God and that intelligent men may be selected from the various countries of the world to organize an international congress whose chief aim will be the promotion of this universal medium of speech.[61]

From a Talk at the Baptist Temple, Philadelphia

Ninth, a universal language shall be adopted and be taught by all the schools and institutions of the world. A committee appointed by national bodies of learning shall select a suitable language to be used as a medium of international communication. All must acquire it. This is one of the great factors in the unification of man.[62]

From a Talk at All Souls Unitarian Church, New York

Diversity of languages has been a fruitful cause of discord. The function of language is to convey the thought and purpose of one to another. Therefore, it matters not what language man speaks or employs. Sixty years ago, Bahá'u'lláh advocated one language as the greatest means of unity and the basis of international conference. He wrote to the kings and rulers of the various nations, recommending that one language should be sanctioned and adopted by all governments. According to this each nation should acquire the universal language in addition to its native tongue. The world would then be in close communication, consultation would become general, and dissensions due to diversity of speech would be removed.[63]

≈

From a Talk at the Church of the Messiah, Montreal

Bahá'u'lláh has proclaimed the adoption of a universal language. A language shall be agreed upon by which unity will be established in the world. Each person will require training in two languages: his native tongue and the universal auxiliary form of speech. This will facilitate intercommunication and dispel the misunderstandings which the barriers of language have occasioned in the world. All people worship the same God and are alike His servants. When they are able to communicate freely, they will associate in friendship and concord, entertain the greatest love and fellowship for each other, and in reality the Orient and Occident will embrace in unity and agreement.[64]

≈

From a Talk at St James Methodist Church, Montreal

Eleventh, one language must be selected as an international medium of speech and communication. Through this means misunderstandings will be lessened, fellowship established, and unity assured.[65]

⌇

From a Talk at the Home of Juliet Thompson, New York

Bahá'u'lláh has announced the necessity for a universal language which shall serve as a means of international communication and thus remove misunderstandings and difficulties. This teaching is set forth in the Kitáb-i-Aqdas ('Most Holy Book') published fifty years ago.[66]

⌇

Answer to a question asked at the Golden Circle Club, Boston

A few weeks ago, I wrote a letter from New York to one of the promoters of Esperanto telling him that this language could become universal if a council of delegates chosen from among the nations and rulers were established which would discuss Esperanto and consider the means to promote it.[67]

⌇

From a Talk given at the Unitarian Church, Montreal

Seventh, a universal language is necessary. A language should be adopted which can be acquired by all. Every person will have to learn two languages – one, his own, and the other, universal, so that all persons will have a means of communication. This will cause the removal of misunderstandings among the various nations. All worship one God and all are the servants of the one God. Differences occur when people cannot understand one another. When they can talk in the same language, differences due to misunderstandings will melt away, while love and harmony will have their sway. The East and the West will then join hands and unite with each other in bonds of union.[68]

IV WRITINGS BY AND ON BEHALF OF SHOGHI EFFENDI

He [Bahá'u'lláh], moreover, in His Most Holy Book, has enjoined the selection of a single language and the adoption of a common script for all on earth to use, an injunction which, when carried out, would, as He Himself affirms in that Book, be one of the signs of the 'coming of age of the human race'.[69]

~

The injunction to 'consort with all men in a spirit of friendliness and fellowship' He [Bahá'u'lláh] further emphasizes, and recognizes such association to be con-ducive to 'union and concord', which, He affirms, are the establishers of order in the world and the quickeners of nations. The necessity of adopting a universal tongue and script He repeatedly stresses; deplores the waste of time involved in the study of divers languages; affirms that with the adoption of such a language and script the whole earth will be considered as 'one city and one land'; and claims to be possessed of the knowledge of both, and ready to impart it to any one who might seek it from Him.[70]

~

A world language will either be invented or chosen from among the existing languages and will be taught in the schools of all the federated nations as an auxiliary to their mother tongue. A world script, a world literature, a uniform and universal system of currency, of weights and measures, will simplify and facilitate intercourse and understanding among the nations and races of mankind.[71]

~

Now with utmost vigour you should make a supreme effort to teach and encourage the spread of Esperanto, for it has assumed great importance, and occupy yourself in the translation of the Writings – in particular the important, general Tablets – forwarding them to this servant so that they may be published. (Letter of 18 October 1925)[72]

~

Should the Eastern friends wish to obtain a degree of mastery of a Western language that would equip them to enter into correspondence with the Western friends, and should the Western friends wish to obtain a similar mastery of an Oriental tongue, for most of them this would prove an arduous and time-consuming task. With Esperanto the case is different as it is an easy language in both its written and spoken forms. Were the friends to learn this language the result would be to engender a greater feeling of love and unity amongst them and to facilitate the promotion of the Teachings revealed for this New Age by the Glorious King. Exert your utmost endeavour, then, in this praiseworthy undertaking, so that you may be instrumental in scattering abroad the fragrances of God's Manifestation and that you may impart joy and gladness to the hearts of the friends. (Letter of 30 January 1926)[73]

~

It has given me the greatest pleasure to receive the first issues of the Bahá'í Esperanto Gazette, and to learn of the splendid start you have made along a path which I am certain will lead you ultimately to glorious and abiding success.

I hail the inauguration of an international Bahá'í Organ, so vitally needed at the present stage of our work, and destined to render services that are unique in their character to the component parts of the ever-expanding Bahá'í world.

Though limited in its sphere of influence, and modest in features, yet it shall, due to the vital position it fulfils, grow from strength to strength and vindicate its claim as the one medium of international Bahá'í intercourse. That it may achieve this purpose, it is incumbent upon those who are responsible for its publication and development to devise ways and means for the establishment and maintenance of regular and frequent communications with the various Bahá'í National Spiritual Assemblies, that in time this promising Magazine may faithfully portray with force and beauty the diverse achievements of Bahá'í communities throughout the world.

I assure you of my deepest interest in this fresh field of Bahá'í enterprise, and of my great desire to promote in such parts of the Bahá'í world as present circumstances permit the study of an international language which is of such an obvious and practical utility to our steadily advancing Cause. (Letter to the editor of *La Nova Tago*)[74]

⌒

My dear fellow-workers in the service of humanity:

I take great pleasure in addressing you, on the occasion

of the opening of the Nineteenth Universal Congress of Esperanto in Danzig, and in wishing you from all my heart the fullest success in the great work you are doing for the promotion of the good of humanity.

It will interest you, I am sure, to learn, that as a result of the repeated and emphatic admonitions of 'Abdu'l-Bahá, His many followers even in the distant villages and hamlets of Persia, where the light of Western civilization has hardly penetrated as yet, as well as in other lands throughout the East, are strenuously and enthusiastically engaged in the study and teaching of Esperanto, for whose future they cherish the highest hopes.

I am voicing the sentiments of the unnumbered followers of the Faith throughout the world, when I offer you through this letter, the cordial expression of our sincere best wishes and fervent prayers for the success of your noble end. (Letter to the Nineteenth Universal Congress of Esperanto, 17 April 1927)[75]

⸱⸱⸱

For the purposes of communication and correspondence between the friends of East and West, this language [Esperanto] and script are both eminently suitable, for, once mastered – which they may be in a short space of time – they will furnish the friends with a medium in which they can exchange news and views, and a means to which they can have recourse in strengthening the ties of love and fellowship between them. (Letter to an individual, 18 May 1927)[76]

⸱⸱⸱

On the occasion of the opening of the Bahá'í Faith Universal Congress of Esperanto, I wish to reaffirm, in the name of the Bahá'ís of both the East and the West, the sentiments of goodwill, fellowship and loving sympathy, that animate the followers of Bahá'u'lláh in their attitude towards the work in which you are so nobly and devotedly engaged.

I can assure you that the members of the worldwide Bahá'í community follow with increasing interest and genuine hope the progress of your labours, and feel that by your high endeavours you are promoting one of the outstanding principles proclaimed by Bahá'u'lláh.

They share with me the fervent hope that in the days to come closer bonds of cooperation and fellowship may bind the Esperantists of the world with our beloved Faith, and that the establishment and maintenance of intimate relationships between Bahá'ís and Esperantists may prove conducive to the betterment of mankind.

May the Almighty guide and bless your deliberations, and graciously assist you to bring into closer understanding and communion the divers peoples and nations of a sorely divided world. (Letter to the Twentieth Universal Congress of Esperanto, 4 May 1928)[77]

He was interested in your efforts to make the English language, which undoubtedly is the most generally spoken and widely understood, the world's auxiliary language, and we must wait and see how other European nations receive it. Of course, as you had well put it, the mere existence of prejudice is no argument against the possibility of making an existing language universal. The world must try to overcome its many defects and not reinforce them. Perhaps the main consideration in the future will be the specific qualities of a language as being exact, rich and easy to learn for both East and West. (Letter of 18 May 1928)[78]

᷍

What Bahá'u'lláh says is that the Supreme House of Justice will appoint a committee that will study the whole matter and then either choose one of the existing languages or create a new one, to function as an international language. The Master never went beyond that, i.e. He never tried to solve the problem Himself and choose that language. He still leaves it to the Supreme House of Justice. But He says that Esperanto will spread and even went so far as to encourage all the friends who possibly can to study it. In fact the knowledge of Esperanto has proven very useful for one who tries to teach in different countries of the world. But whether Esperanto will become the international language which is to be a part of our religious and social duties to study, no one knows, and we have no evidence that the Master made any definite statement along that line. The Master has scarcely ever assumed the solution of a problem that Bahá'u'lláh has referred to the Supreme House of Justice. Esperanto may become *an* international language, but it depends upon the House of Justice to choose it as *the* international language. And no one is in a position to foretell. (Letter of 30 August 1928)[79]

᷍

Shoghi Effendi wishes me to acknowledge the receipt of your letter dated August 18th 1930 and to express his deep appreciation for the work you as well as the other friends achieved at the Esperanto Congress held in Oxford. He hopes that your efforts will bear great fruits and bring many souls to a true appreciation of the Cause. He hopes that as a result of the activities of the Bahá'í Esperantists that society will come to know that before long they will have to merge their limited ideal of one auxiliary language into the greater and more universal ideal of one united world, under the banner and teachings of Bahá'u'lláh. Meanwhile Shoghi Effendi hopes that you will keep in touch, either through correspondence or otherwise, with those who have been interested and make them accept the Cause in its entirety. (Letter of 19 September 1930)[80]

⤸

The Bahá'ís have always considered with deep interest and esteem the wonderful work the Esperantists are achieving in putting into practice one of the foremost principles of their Faith. Many of their numbers have been encouraged to study that language and participate in promoting its many interests. They would therefore be very willing to cooperate with you in matters that are of mutual interest . . . May God hasten the day when your hopes as well as ours will be realized. (Letter of 14 March 1932)[81]

⤸

There is a strong bond which unites the Bahá'ís and the Esperantists, since they are both striving to create a world community in which linguistic differences will cease to separate peoples and nations, but will rather serve to foster among them the spirit of service, and of good-will. May Bahá'u'lláh enable you to strengthen this bond of amity and cooperation through your continued participation in all Esperantist meetings and congresses, so that you may spread His Message with increasing vigour and success. (Letter of 30 August 1933)[82]

He wishes me particularly to convey to you his most genuine appreciation of your services in connection with the publication of 'La Nova Tago' which he hopes will, through your efforts and those of the Esperanto-speaking Bahá'ís both in Germany and abroad, develop gradually into a leading Esperanto review, and thus become an effective medium for the spread of Teachings in Esperantist circles throughout the world. It is in view of the far-reaching possibilities which this publication can have as a teaching organ, that he has urged the German N.S.A. to resume its publication when, a few months ago, they had almost decided to discontinue printing it.

With regard to your request for a special article from the Guardian which you wish to have published in the forthcoming issue of your magazine. He would suggest that you should translate his general letter addressed to the friends a few years ago, entitled 'The Goal of a New World Order', as this, he feels, is a very suitable material for publication in that review, and is by far better than anything he can write at present.

As to your suggestion regarding a more widespread use of the Esperanto among the Bahá'ís as a medium of correspondence. Shoghi Effendi, as you know, has been invariable encouraging the believers, both in the East and in the West, to make an intensive study of that language, and to consider it as an important medium for the spread of the Cause in international circles. He has been specially urging the friends to have the Cause well represented in all Esperanto Congresses and associations, and by this means cultivate greater friendship and cooperation between them and the Esperantists.

But in this connection, he feels, he must make it clear that although the Cause views with much sympathy and appreciation the activities which the Esperantists are increasingly initiating for the spread of their language, yet it considers that the adoption of Esperanto by the entire world is by no means an *inevitable* fact. Neither Bahá'u'lláh, nor even 'Abdu'l-Bahá, ever stated that Esperanto will be *the* international auxiliary language. The Master simply expressed the *hope* that it may, provided certain conditions were fulfilled, develop into such a medium. (Letter of 3 August 1935)[83]

⤚

Concerning your study of Esperanto: the Guardian does not feel it advisable that you get too busy introducing any changes in that language, as this is not only a type of activity for which you are not qualified, but is also void of any use or advantage as far as your Bahá'í work is concerned, in view of the fact that it is by no means certain that Esperanto will necessarily develop into the world auxiliary language referred to by Bahá'u'lláh in His writings. (Letter of 17 April 1936)[84]

⤚

Concerning the study of Esperanto: it would be very helpful indeed if the friends would study that language, not so much because of the possibilities it has to develop into the international auxiliary language of the future (we have no statement from either Bahá'u'lláh or 'Abdu'l-Bahá to the effect that it will develop into such a language) but chiefly as a helpful medium for the spread of the Cause. (Letter of 5 May 1936)[85]

∾

Regarding the teaching of Esperanto: the Guardian thoroughly appreciates the efforts you are exerting for the spread of this language . . . He wishes me, however, to bring to your attention the fact that neither Bahá'u'lláh nor 'Abdu'l-Bahá did specifically state that Esperanto would certainly become the international auxiliary language of the future, neither did they enjoin its teaching upon the believers. What 'Abdu'l-Bahá chiefly did was to highly praise it, and to reveal its possibilities. The teaching of Esperanto is, therefore, not a command or an obligation in the sense that praying is, for instance. What is enjoined by Bahá'u'lláh is either the creation of a new language, or the adoption of one of the existing languages for use as an international medium of communication. Let us hope that Esperanto may someday develop into such a medium. (Letter of 26 December 1936)[86]

∾

Regarding the subject of Esperanto: it should be made clear to the believers that while the teaching of that language has been repeatedly encouraged by 'Abdu'l-Bahá, there is no reference either from Him or from Bahá'u'lláh that can make us believe that it will necessarily develop into the international auxiliary language of the future. Bahá'u'lláh has specified in His writings that such a language will either have to be chosen from one of the existing languages, or an entirely new one should be created to serve as a medium of exchange between the nations and peoples of the world. Pending this final choice, the Bahá'ís are advised to study Esperanto only on consideration of the fact that the learning of this language can considerably facilitate inter-communication between individuals, groups, and Assemblies throughout the Bahá'í world in the present stage of the evolution of the Faith. (Letter of 4 June 1937)[87]

⌒

Now with reference to your question regarding the meaning of the passage on page 25 of the 'Epistle to the Son of the Wolf': the science referred to is hidden in the knowledge of Bahá'u'lláh.

As to the new tongue and script to which Bahá'u'lláh refers on page 107 of that same book: we do not know to what particular medium of language they refer.

Concerning Esperanto: it is uncertain whether it will develop into the international auxiliary language of the future. (Letter of 9 August 1937)[88]

⌒

You complain that the believers in America do not attach sufficient importance to the study of Esperanto; this may be true, and is partly due to the fact that they do no longer believe that it will *necessarily* develop into the international auxiliary language of the future. The interest which the Bahá'ís have and should have in this language is essentially because of the vital significance of the idea it represents rather than the belief in its *inherent* worth as a suitable and adequate international medium of expression.

The Bahá'ís indeed welcome Esperanto as the first experiment of its kind in modern times. They are in full sympathy with the Esperantists in so far as they stress the absolute necessity for the creation of an international language to be studied by all the peoples of the world in addition to their respective national languages.

The Guardian himself would have learned it, but his occupations are so manifold and overwhelming that he cannot possibly find the time to do so. (Letter of 31 October 1937)[89]

One thing, however, the Guardian feels the believers should be very careful to avoid in all such contacts with the Esperantists: namely that of giving them the impression that they consider Esperanto as necessarily constituting that international auxiliary language of the future referred to by Bahá'u'lláh and stressed by Him as an indispensable element in the upbuilding of the coming New World Order.

To give them such a false conception of the true Bahá'í attitude regarding the choice of the future world international language would not only be an act of dishonesty and disloyalty towards the Cause, but would lead to serious misunderstandings and misapprehensions, and eventually result in counteracting the effect of any temporary gains or advantages which may accrue to the Faith through such association and contact with the Esperantists.

It is not so much that language as the central idea it embodies and inculcates which the Bahá'ís endorse, and only through keeping firm to such an attitude can they hope to establish any fruitful and enduring contacts with various Esperanto groups and associations throughout the world. (Letter of 24 April 1939)[90]

∽

We have no authentic record of 'Abdu'l-Bahá in which He states that Esperanto will be the universal language of the future. It may be Esperanto, it may be some other language, we do not know; but as we believe so firmly in the necessity of an international language, we are always eager to cooperate with the Esperantists. (Letter of 25 January 1943)[91]

∽

Regarding your question of 'Basic English's' usefulness as an international language: He is not very familiar with it, as he is too preoccupied with the tremendous amount of work he has to do here. But what little he has read about it makes him doubt whether it would ever be adequate to meet the requirements of an auxiliary tongue. (Letter of 30 June 1944)[92]

∽

Regarding the whole question of an international language and its relation to the Faith: We, as Bahá'ís, are very anxious to see a universal auxiliary tongue adopted as soon as possible; we are not the protagonists of any one language to fill this post. If the Governments of the world should agree on an existing language, or a constructed, new tongue, to be used internationally, we would heartily support it because we desire to see this step in the unification of the human race take place as soon as possible.

Esperanto has been in wide use, more so than any similar language, all over the world, and the Bahá'ís have been encouraged by both the Master and the Guardian to learn it and to translate Bahá'í literature into it. We cannot be sure it will be the chosen international language of the future; but as it is the one which has spread the most, both East and West, we should certainly continue to cooperate with its members, learn to speak it and translate Bahá'í literature into it.

He feels you can rest assured that 'Abdu'l-Bahá's statement, made in Paris, was prompted by His insight and wisdom and not due to the opinions of anyone else.

Naturally the money of the Cause should not be spent on translating and publishing literature in international languages that have no following worth mentioning! (Letter of 17 October 1944)[93]

꩜

He feels that the subject of the Bahá'í work in Esperanto in Germany is a matter for you to take up with the National Spiritual Assembly; we Bahá'ís do not claim Esperanto *will* be the auxiliary language of the future – but, as we firmly believe in the necessity of an auxiliary language we are glad to support this work by publishing books in Esperanto and encouraging the Bahá'ís to learn it, if they wish to.[94]

⤳

Regarding your questions about the Esperantists: for many years they have been one of our closest contacts in Europe, and many of them have become believers. They are working for one of our greatest principles, and we certainly should associate with them. In Germany the Bahá'ís published an Esperanto magazine, and Martha Root represented the Cause at Esperanto congresses. We cannot say we are sure this language will be the international one, but we are anxious to see it spread as it fosters unity and understanding. By all means foster your contact with them. Whether Esperanto will be chosen as the international language or not we cannot say, but we can say we hope it will spread because it nearly fulfils such a noble purpose. (Letter of 5 April 1947)[95]

⤳

The Guardian has frequently urged the Bahá'ís to not only associate with Esperantists but learn to speak Esperanto. On the other hand, we cannot, as Bahá'ís, officially claim that we believe Esperanto should, or will, become the universal auxiliary language. What we are interested in is that a language should become universally used in order to hasten peace and co-operation among the nations; we do not care which one it is, just as we do not care which monetary system is universally adopted, etc. This does not mean, however, that the Bahá'ís should not study Esperanto and co-operate in a friendly way with the Esperanto Society.

Esperantists should realize that we are a religion, not a society, and that we are, according to the broad principles and instructions of our Faith, seeking to usher in a new World Order. We are, in this sense, intensely liberal; we do not espouse the plans of other societies, even though their aims may be in some respects the same as ours; we co-operate with them, gladly, but, except for our specific teachings, we do not seek to make others adopt any particular system, however progressive it may be. This is our attitude towards Esperanto.

For official Bahá'í correspondence to be carried on in Esperanto would be impossible, as the vast majority of Bahá'ís the world over speak either English or Persian, and the Guardian's correspondence is in these two languages. Whenever a language is adopted by the nations of the world as the international medium, no doubt we too will adopt and use it. If it should happen to be Esperanto we would be very pleased of our long and friendly association with Esperantists and the great contribution their language has already made to a better understanding amongst peoples. The Guardian can, therefore, only reiterate what he has often said: that the Bahá'ís should study Esperanto and co-operate with that Society, but we cannot say this is the universal language we adopt! (Letter of 31 March 1948)[96]

∽

Neither the Master, nor the Guardian, has stated English would be the universal language. (Letter of 25 March 1949)[97]

∽

V Texts by and on behalf of the Universal House of Justice

A fundamental lack of communication between peoples seriously undermines efforts towards world peace. Adopting an international auxiliary language would go far to resolving this problem and necessitates the most urgent attention. (*The Promise of World Peace*)[98]

꩜

Bahá'u'lláh enjoins the adoption of a universal language and script. His Writings envisage two stages in this process. The first stage is to consist of the selection of an existing language or an invented one which would then be taught in all the schools of the world as an auxiliary to the mother tongues. The governments of the world through their parliaments are called upon to effect this momentous enactment. The second stage, in the distant future, would be the eventual adoption of one single language and common script for all on earth.[99]

꩜

The United Nations, which currently uses six official languages, would derive substantial benefit from either choosing a single existing language or creating a new one to be used as an auxiliary language in all its fora. Such a step has long been advocated by many groups, from the Esperantists to the Bahá'í International Community itself. In addition to saving money and simplifying bureaucratic procedures, such a move would go far toward promoting a spirit of unity.

We propose the appointment of a high-level Commission, with members from various regions and drawn from relevant fields, including linguistics, economics, the social sciences, education and the media, to begin careful study on the matter of an international auxiliary language and the adoption of a common script.

We foresee that eventually, the world cannot but adopt a single, universally agreed-upon auxiliary language and script to be taught in schools worldwide, as a supplement to the language or languages of each country. The objective would be to facilitate the transition to a global society through better communication among nations, reduction of administrative costs for businesses, governments and others involved in global enterprise, and a general fostering of more cordial relations between all members of the human family.

This proposal should be read narrowly. It does not in any way envision the decline of any living language or culture. (*Turning Point for All Nations*)[100]

∽

While it will be decades – or perhaps a great deal longer – before the vision contained in this remarkable document (The Seven Candles of Unity) is fully realized, the essential features of what it promised are now established facts throughout the world. In several of the great changes envisioned – unity of race and unity of religion – the intent of the Master's words is clear and the processes involved are far advanced, however great may be the resistance in some quarters. To a large extent this is also true of unity of language. The need for it is now recognized on all sides, as reflected in the circumstances that have compelled the United Nations and much of the non-governmental community to adopt several 'official languages'. Until a decision is taken by international agreement, the effect of such developments as the Internet, the management of air traffic, the development of technological vocabularies of various kinds, and universal education itself, has been to make it possible, to some extent, for English to fill the gap. (*Century of Light*)[101]

⌒

Your letter of 9 'Aẓamat, 128 expressing your feeling that the endorsement by the Universal House of Justice of an international auxiliary language for Bahá'í conventions would not prejudice any future World Government in its choice of a world-wide tongue for official use, and that Esperanto is widely used by clerical, businessmen's, and scientific conventions, has been received.

Regarding your first comment, inasmuch as Bahá'u-'lláh has said that the Supreme House of Justice will appoint a committee that will study the whole matter and then either choose one of the existing languages or create a new one to function as an international language, when such a choice shall have been made, the action will automatically constitute an endorsement of the chosen auxiliary language.

With reference to Esperanto, we share with you an excerpt from a letter written on behalf of the beloved Guardian by his secretary to an individual in 1937:

The interest which Bahá'ís have and should have in this language is essentially because of the vital significance of the idea it represents rather than the belief in its inherent worth as a suitable and adequate international medium of expression.

The Bahá'ís indeed welcome Esperanto as the first experiment of its kind in modern times. They are in full sympathy with the Esperantists in so far as they stress the absolute necessity for the creation of an international language to be studied by all the peoples of the world in addition to their respective national languages.

As to the most propitious time for the choosing of an international auxiliary language, we feel that it is not feasible for the House of Justice to make the choice at this time. (Letter of 8 June 1971)[102]

In reply to the suggestion contained in your letter of 11 Rahmat that the beloved Guardian's extensive study and use of English may be 'used as a confirmation to the use of English as the universal auxiliary language' we must advise you that such an assumption is quite unwarranted.

At the present time no one can say what the future international language and/or script may be. (Letter of 20 July 1972)[103]

As English and Persian are the two official languages

of the Universal House of Justice we regret that we cannot write to you in Esperanto but we will be glad to enclose an Esperanto translation of our letter for you in view of the fact that you do not understand English well. We hope that it will be possible for Mr Habibullah Taherzadeh to make such translations if his time allows.

With regard to the enquiry in your letter of 11 Jalál, our understanding of the aim of the Bahaa Esperanto-Ligo when we agreed to its formation was that it was to be an official non-neutral department of the Universal Esperanto Association comprising those Esperantists who are also Bahá'ís with the aim of encouraging collaboration among such friends and promoting the Bahá'í teachings among their fellow Esperantists.

While individual Bahá'í Esperantists are, of course, free to encourage their fellow Bahá'ís to study Esperanto, this should not be an activity of the Bahaa Esperanto-Ligo, and it should be borne in mind that whereas it is clear that the Bahá'í Faith upholds the principle of an international auxiliary language, no decision as to which language this shall be has yet been made. (Letter of May 1974)[104]

of

Further to our letter to you of 2 December 1974, and with reference to your question on the world language, the Universal House of Justice has asked us to draw your attention to the statement of Bahá'u'lláh in the Eighth Leaf of the Exalted Paradise (in *Bahá'í World Faith*, p. 182): 'We have formerly declared that speech was decreed to be in two languages, and that there should be an effort to reduce it into one.'

When the beloved Guardian was asked by an individual believer about the meaning of this passage, his secretary gave the following reply on his behalf:

> What Bahá'u'lláh is referring to in the Eighth Leaf of the Exalted Paradise is a far distant time, when the world is really one country, and one language would be a sensible possibility. It does not contradict His instructions as to the need immediately for an auxiliary language. (Letter of 29 December 1974)[105]

↬

The House of Justice instructs us to say in reply to Mr . . .'s letter to the Local Spiritual Assembly of . . . that he should be advised that the time has not yet come for the Universal House of Justice to take any such step as he suggests. There is no doubt of the vital importance of the establishment of a universal language and it will inevitably come about but the believers have more urgent matters to attend to at the present and are asked to concentrate on teaching the Cause and winning the goals of the Five Year Plan. (Letter of 2 March 1976)[106]

↬

The House of Justice realizes that you must sometimes be faced with somewhat embarrassing situations in relation to your fellow-Esperantists since, as Bahá'ís, you are fully aware that, for all its undoubted qualities, Esperanto may well not be the international language that is ultimately chosen, and that it is the concept of an international language that the Bahá'ís are enthusiastic in supporting rather than any particular solution to the problem.

The Guardian's advice that Bahá'ís must be entirely open about this matter in relation to Esperantists so as to avoid serious misunderstandings and misapprehensions in the future will no doubt be of great assistance to you in your work and enable you to forge ahead with full enthusiasm without, in any way, appearing to sail under false colours. (Letter of 6 October 1976)[107]

⌒

Your letter of May 23 to the Universal House of Justice regarding a suggested solution for a universal auxiliary language has been received and we are asked to transmit its advice.

The thought that a form of sign language might fulfil the requirements for a universal auxiliary language is not a new one to students of language and human communication, who have studied many alternatives. Suffice it to say that the limitations of sign language far exceed their apparent merits, appealing as some aspects of such systems may be. In any event, the time has not yet come for the adoption of the universal language as called for by the Faith, although it is timely to continue the preparatory studies which may be the basis for rational international consultation and ultimate adoption of one language for the world.

You are doubtless aware that there are many Bahá'ís who are enthusiasts of the world language movements, including many who are Esperantists. Through our United Nations activities the Bahá'ís are vigilant in monitoring all initiatives which may lead to this vital objective of a common language for a world society.

The House of Justice encourages the interest of the

believers in all the great principles of the Cause which together will ultimately bring world unity, and it hopes that your concern for the Faith of God will continue to be stimulated in such fruitful directions. (Letter of 6 July 1977)[108]

῀

You are quite correct in stating that there are two different provisions in the Sacred Texts for the selection of an International Auxiliary Language. On the one hand, this task is given to the governments of the world, on the other it is given to the House of Justice. It is not possible now to foresee exactly how this will come about, but it would seem reasonable to suppose that, long before the Bahá'í community is large enough or can exercise the authority to produce such a world-embracing change, events will compel the governments, either progressively or all in concert, to select an International Auxiliary Language to be taught as a second language in all schools and to be used in all international commerce. At a much later stage, possibly at the time of the Bahá'í World Commonwealth, the Universal House of Justice may well decide to review the situation and either confirm the decision that the governments had made, or change the choice to a more suitable language.

Of course, conditions may produce a development very different from the one just outlined. One of the characteristics of Bahá'í Administration is its flexibility which enables it to deal with unforeseen developments and continually changing conditions. The one certain thing about the choice of an International Auxiliary Language is that the Universal House of Justice does not judge the present time propitious for it to take any action in this regard. (Letter of 8 June 1980)[109]

⟿

It is not yet timely for the House of Justice to make a pronouncement in favour of any particular language – the important thing now, in this particular field, is for Bahá'ís to promote the principle. Learning Esperanto, or one of the other proposed auxiliary languages, brings one into touch with people all over the world who are conscious of the need, who are internationally minded, and who may well be attracted to the Faith. Therefore, if you have a particular interest in this subject and an inclination to study Esperanto, you should feel no inhibitions about doing so. (Letter of 2 June 1982)[110]

⟿

The difficulties of international communication in a polyglot world are strikingly evident to any Bahá'í who has gone travel teaching to foreign lands or has attended international conferences. The Universal House of Justice feels that for it to choose any language for the Bahá'ís to use as an international auxiliary language would give rise to greater difficulties than would thereby be solved at the present time. The friends, however, remembering that this is one of the very important principles of the Faith, would do well to support the concept whenever possible, and to pray that the time is not far removed when the governments of the nations will adopt a single language to be taught in all the schools of the world as an auxiliary to the pupils' mother-tongue. (*The Principle of an International Auxiliary Language*)[111]

〜

As to your enquiries about a universal auxiliary language and a world script, the House of Justice asks us to say that it knows of nothing in the letters or writings of Shoghi Effendi about the creation of an orthography for an international auxiliary language or of a treatise on Arabic as possibly such a language. (Letter of 26 March 1986)[112]

〜

In spite of its virtues, however, and of the encouragement given to Bahá'ís to study it, Esperanto cannot with certainty be hailed as the international language which the peoples of the world will eventually adopt . . .

For its own use the Universal House of Justice has adopted the two languages used for the most part by the beloved Guardian, namely English and Persian. It also has translators who provide translations of its letters into Spanish and French for the believers in the large areas of the world where these two languages are dominant. Until now the Universal House of Justice has felt that the introduction of an international auxiliary language within the Bahá'í community for the purposes you describe, would place too great a burden on the believers, many of whom are already compelled to learn one or more foreign languages to operate in the societies in which they live. (Letter of 17 June 1986)[113]

〜

We feel that, within the framework of their efforts for the promotion of peace, the Bahá'ís of Europe would do well to increase their collaboration with the Esperanto Movement, and we encourage Bahá'ís who feel the urge to assist in this area to learn Esperanto and take an active part in the activities of the Movement. As you know, although both 'Abdu'l-Bahá and Shoghi Effendi have made it clear that it is by no means certain that Esperanto will eventually be chosen as the international auxiliary language of the world, 'Abdu'l-Bahá encouraged the friends in the East and the West to learn it as a practical step in the promotion of the concept of the adoption of an international auxiliary language to break down the barriers to understanding between peoples.

Thus, as the followers of Bahá'u'lláh are collaborating with many different individuals and associations in the promotion of projects of economic and social development and towards the establishment of world peace, some of them should make a point of active collaboration with the Esperantists who, they will find, share many ideals with them. (Letter of 17 September 1986)[114]

On behalf of the members of the Bahá'í community in every land, we extend to you, and through you to all members of the Universal Esperanto Association, our heartfelt congratulations on the approaching centenary of Esperanto.

The creation of Esperanto was welcomed wholeheartedly by 'Abdu'l-Bahá as a major step in the establishment of an international auxiliary language, which had been called for by Bahá'u'lláh, the Founder of the Bahá'í Faith, and its continuing progress is an important element in the worldwide acceptance of the oneness of mankind in practice as well as in theory.

Your illustrious founder, Dr. Ludwig Zamenhof, is honoured by Bahá'ís in every land, both for his magnificent achievement in creating Esperanto as well as for his deeply felt humanitarian ideals. The acceptance of the Bahá'í Faith by his daughter, Lidia, cemented even more firmly the bonds of close association between our two movements. At this moment, therefore, we rejoice with you all, and extend to you our warmest good wishes for the continuing and increasing success of all your efforts. (Letter of 30 June 1987)[115]

꘏

As to your question about the possibility of English becoming the international auxiliary language, the Universal House of Justice, in its reply dated 20 July 1972 to an individual believer, who had suggested that the beloved Guardian's extensive study and use of the English language may be seen as a confirmation that this language would be used as the universal auxiliary language, stated that such an assumption is quite unwarranted and that, at the present time, no one can say what the future international language and/or script may be. (Letter of 2 August 1990)[116]

꘏

Much as the Universal House of Justice appreciates the great value that Esperanto has for international communication, and the highly significant role that it has played and will undoubtedly continue to play in the work of teaching the Faith . . . it does not deem it advisable to carry out Mr . . . .'s recommendation.

The need for the adoption of an international auxiliary language is clearly pressing, and was frequently stressed by Bahá'u'lláh. However, the House of Justice is not in a position at this time to indicate that any particular language should be adopted. Nevertheless, in view of the many close associations between the Bahá'í community and the Esperanto Movement which have existed for many decades, and in light of the extraordinary strides which Esperanto has made, the House of Justice welcomed the formation of the Bahaa Esperanto-Ligo and such national Bahá'í Esperanto associations as BELusono, whose members, through their many and widespread activities, are rendering outstanding services in promoting the consciousness of the need for an international auxiliary language, in demonstrating its effectiveness, and, at the same time, in disseminating the message of Bahá'u'lláh among so many people of diverse races and backgrounds who are inspired with the same universal vision. (Letter of 21 December 1990)[117]

⌒

Although there is no doubt that the English language is widely accepted as an international means of communication, particularly in business and trade, science and technology, as well as in international affairs, it has not been adopted by the world as the international language.

In response to a similar inquiry, our Department had been instructed to point out that there are two different provisions in the Sacred Texts for the selection of an international auxiliary language, namely, that on the one hand, this task is given to the governments of the world, and on the other it is given to the Universal House of Justice, as indicated in the following references:

In the Tablet of Bishárát, Bahá'u'lláh states the following: 'It behoveth the sovereigns of the world – may God assist them – or the ministers of the earth to take counsel together and to adopt one of the existing languages or a new one to be taught to children in schools throughout the world, and likewise one script. Thus the whole earth will come to be regarded as one country.'

In the Tablet of Ishráqát, He states: 'In former Epistles We have enjoined upon the Trustees of the House of Justice either to choose one language from among those now existing or to adopt a new one, and in like manner to select a common script, both of which should be taught in all the schools of the world.'

Regarding the former quotation there is no doubt that current and future events will certainly compel the governments of the world to adopt an international language. As to the latter passage, the time has not yet come for the Universal House of Justice to make any pronouncements on this issue. (Letter of 5 September 1991)[118]

This is to acknowledge with thanks receipt of your letter dated 29 December 1993 and materials enclosed therein regarding the international language Glosa. We are requested to provide the following reply.

As you are already aware, the Universal House of Justice has made no pronouncements as to which language will be selected as the international auxiliary tongue to be adopted by the peoples of the world. Even in relation to the highly visible international language Esperanto 'Abdu'l-Bahá and Shoghi Effendi encouraged the believers to support its associations not because Bahá'ís feel it will be chosen as the auxiliary language, but because we champion the principle of the need for such a language in the future world civilization.

While Bahá'ís are therefore free to engage in initiatives like Glosa or like-minded associations whose aims are to promote the idea of an international auxiliary language, they will also no doubt want to weigh the time commitment that any such undertakings would involve against the opportunities they feel would consequently arise for them to share the Cause of Bahá'u'lláh with individuals naturally inclined toward the concept of a unified world. (Letter of 12 January 1994)[119]

∽

The creation of a world language would undoubtedly require research of an enormous scope, and the House of Justice does not feel that it would be timely, given the pressing tasks of the Four Year Plan, to call upon Bahá'ís generally to mount an effort such as you have described, which attempts to resolve or address some of the practical issues related to such an undertaking. More urgent is the necessity for promoting the idea, in principle, of an international auxiliary language. (Letter of 11 November 1996)[120]

∽

. . . the Research Department feels it might be pertinent to highlight some points made in a letter dated 8 June 1980 written on behalf of the Universal House of Justice . . .

From a careful reading of this passage, we have drawn the following points which the League may wish to review:

- The process leading to the final selection of the International Auxiliary Language may well proceed in stages.

- The first stage may coincide with the period 'long before the Bahá'í community is large enough or can exercise the authority to produce such a world-embracing change', when it is likely to be 'events' (and not the Bahá'ís) which 'compel' governments to select an International Auxiliary Language to be taught as a second language in schools, and to be used in 'international commerce'.

- During this first stage, governments might make the selection of this language 'either progressively or all in concert'.

- A second 'much later' stage is also alluded to, 'possibly at the time of the Bahá'í World Commonwealth', when the Universal House of Justice 'may well decide to review the situation and either confirm the decision that the governments have made, or change the choice to a more suitable language'.

- Another point made in the passage quoted above

which appears to be relevant is that while 'conditions may produce a development very different' from the one outlined here, it is the 'flexibility' of Bahá'í administration 'which enables it to deal with unforeseen developments and continually changing conditions'.

Finally, the Universal House of Justice 'does not judge the present time propitious for it to take any action' regarding the International Auxiliary Language. (Memorandum of the Research Department, 1997)[121]

The tenth principle is the establishment of a universal language so that we shall not have to acquire so many languages in the future. In schools they will study two, the mother tongue and the international auxiliary language. The use of an international auxiliary language will become a great means of dispelling the differences between nations. (Attributed to 'Abdu'l-Bahá)[123]

❧

He ['Abdu'l-Bahá] was asked whether Arabic might become the universal language. He said that it would not. He was then asked about Esperanto. He replied:

A few weeks ago, I wrote a letter from New York to one of the promoters of Esperanto telling him that this language could become universal if a council of delegates chosen from among the nations and rulers were established which would discuss Esperanto and consider the means to promote it. (Attributed to 'Abdu'l-Bahá)[124]

❧

We observe that today the means of unity are brought about. This in itself is evidence that the divine confirmations are with us. One of the principles of the oneness of the world of humanity is the invention of the universal auxiliary language . . . We observe that this language [Esperanto] is spreading daily, and its advocates are increasing. It is indubitable that the universal auxiliary language will become instrumental in wiping away the present misunderstandings, and each individual will be able to be informed of the thought of all humanity.

Therefore we must all strive to spread among our fellow men this language. This international auxiliary language will be an introduction to the establishment of the oneness of the world of humanity. The greatest efforts must be displayed in this direction. (Attributed to 'Abdu'l-Bahá)[125]

~

A Visit to 'Abdu'l-Bahá

'In what way,' I asked him, 'do you think that an international language will help the common peace?'

'Through the facilitation of international relations. When people know each other better, they will also come to understand each other more deeply. They will recognize that, under different clothing, people are the same, that our religions have much in common: the Muslims, for example, are much closer to the Christians than is generally believed. Because of the differences of languages, we see chiefly the differences of beliefs, customs, of desires, but when, along with our native languages, we will have a second common language, we will also see the true, essential similarity among all of them. In the East, for example, and in North Africa, the communality of the Arabic language dispelled for the most part the former distrust, the unrest, that resulted particularly from diversity of languages. The same will occur when all nations and races will be able to use the same language.'

'Will Oriental people learn Esperanto easily?'

'Yes. They learn English or French quickly enough; why, then, would they find great difficulties in Esperanto, which is much easier?'

'Do you think that the Bahá'ís will take favourably to learning our language on your advice?'

'Yes. It cannot, of course, be their paramount concern. But because they will understand the importance of a common language for the realization of our ideal, they will certainly obey my instructions with joy and work for the spread of Esperanto not only in the East but also in the United States of America, where our followers are numerous.'

'Have you already met many Esperantists during your voyage?'

'Yes. They received me very graciously in Edinburgh and two or three days ago right here in Paris. I am now intending to travel to Germany, where I will also likely visit them. They are very sympathetic to me.'

'Another thing: What should be our attitudes towards unjust attacks? Must we be silent, or rebut them?'

'We must simply say the truth, but never attack and particularly never at all seek out personal vengeance. If someone were to kill my son, I would have no right whatsoever to murder the criminal. To do justice through punishment is the duty of society, not of the individual.'

'But if society remains indifferent?'

'We must wait peacefully. In the end, truth, good, and justice will prevail, and peace will triumph!'

At these words I asked his leave to go. 'Abdu'l-Bahá bade me farewell, with a friendly thanks for my sympathy toward his young countryman, because, although persecuted in his fatherland, 'he loves it with all his heart'. (Cart, 'Vizito al Abdul Baha')[126]

∽

Miss Str.: 'Abbas Effendi, may I put this question to the Master of the Bahá'ís: Why has your Prophet Bahá'u'lláh recommended to His followers, besides their respective mother tongue, a world-unifying language, be it Volapük or Esperanto or whatever all the artificially created languages may be called? Is not our English language already a true world language? On the British Empire the sun never sets! With English alone one can travel in five continents without needing another language! Why, therefore, should mankind take the trouble of learning a difficult artificial language besides the mother tongue and besides the English world language?

'Abdu'l-Bahá: O my sister, through your mouth speaks the mighty pride of the British. Consider for once, does not each person love the language of his tribe, or his people, the tongue of his fathers, the mother tongue of his homeland? You surely know how great is the power of linguistic understanding – you yourself mention with praise that one can travel in all continents with 'English' alone! Thus, for world peace and world unity, a common bond of mental understanding, e.g. a world-unifying language, is urgently needed, thus the learned and the laity of all nations are agreed. But if our Blessed Perfection, Bahá'u'lláh, – may His memory be praised – had recommended a language already existing, such as your English, then the representatives of the cultured nations in particular: the Germans, French, Italians, Spaniards, Slavs, Hungarians etc., would have resisted, but even more would the representatives of the Oriental peoples have done so. We, they would say, do not want to learn from childhood the language of the conquerors of the world, by so doing we bend in advance to the British yoke, which we hope one far-distant day to shake off.

Shall I explain this to you with the aid of our precious Persian mother tongue? Well, hear then, my friends:

Our oldest language is 'Zend' which is closely related to the Indian Sanskrit. The holy books of the Avesta (Book of the Teachings of Zoroaster) are written in 'Zend'. During the period of history of the Parthians from 400 B.C. until 300 A.D. (namely during the 'dark 700 years'), the time-honoured language of the 'Avesta' declined. The 'Zend' deteriorated into a mixture with neighbouring languages. Under the rule of the Sassanids the Aramaic language of the Near East displaced all the other language mixtures and combined with the Old Persian to a new language structure, the 'Pahlavi' or 'Huzvaresh', which became the living language of the peoples of the entire central and western Persian realm. In Eastern Persia the Old Persian stood its ground better against the invading Aramaic language element – it developed into 'Parsi', into the real colloquial language, the New Persian. Even the Arab foreign domination, which through the Teachings of Muhammad pushed back the ancient Faith of Zoroaster, of light and fire worshippers, was unable to prevent the reflorescence of the national language of Persian culture. As long as the Persian language of Pahlavi and Parsi ruled, the national epic and the Persian Syrili also flourished in its original and unsullied purity. But in the 11th century the Arabic language penetrated more and

more into the administration and into the upper classes
of the courts, the learned and the merchants. Arabic
was the holy language, the world language of Islam, the
language of the heart of the Prophet Muhammad, the
Messenger of God. Had not the angel of the Highest,
Gabriel, used the Arabic language in charging the Holy
One of God, the Prophet Muhammad, with His worldwide Mission, the proclamation of the 'One God'? The
equalizing power of a mixture of languages, of the pen-
etration into Persian of Arabic elements, made itself
felt from now on. Soon after the brilliant light, Firdawsi,
the purity of the Persian language was lost, the latter
absorbed numerous Arabic foreign words, which it
nationalized and assimilated only in the course of centuries – to the detriment of the Persian epic and lyric.
In the cloak of the modern Persian-Arabic language
pure poetry changed into fashionable rhyming, into
courtly doggerels of praise; an empty content is offered
in an outwardly beautiful form. O my friends, let us
not delude ourselves: language is the most profound
symbol of a people, nay, language is the vestment of the
spirit of a people, language is the measure of the level
of the culture of a nation. An uncontrolled mixing of
languages soon affects the art and then the morale of
the people.

What is barbarism? Barbarism is the unrestricted
domination of unbridled impulses. If the vernacular
language shows slovenliness and arbitrariness, and is
subordinated to the language of the material or spiritual conquerors and victors, it becomes the death-knell
of the freedom of a people! The spiritual history of each
people, be it occidental or oriental, ancient or modern,
proves this. The rebirth of a people, the recovery of its

freedom, begins with the discipline and cultivation of its linguistic heritage. A people which defaces its ancient vestment of language with the spangles borrowed from a foreign language, will live – nay – vegetate on a descending curve. If the Blessed Perfection Bahá'u'lláh is in favour of a world language, this world-unifying language should not darken the wonder of one's own language or displace it. We, the Persian Bahá'í s, do not wish to either give up or urge on others our own language, which developed over thousands of years and is the living testimony of our battles and sufferings, our spiritual defeats and victories.

Take heed, O daughters of the Occident: The cultivation of one's mother tongue is a service to our brethren among our own people. The learning and the use of a world-unifying language, such as Esperanto, is a service to one's brethren among mankind.

One's own language is the native air of which we have need in life and death, which surrounds us from the cradle to the grave, which is and will remain our most personal possession. The world-unifying language is to be compared to a bridge to the rest of the world, to a steam-horse of traffic, an airship for the transport of people and goods.

If you, O man, give up your own, your mother tongue, faith, love and hope will leave you, arts and sciences will desert you, justice and law, morality and ethics will vanish.

What causes the Jews in fact and in truth to be homeless in the wide world – the loss of their Hebrew mother tongue. This is why they begin the reconstruction of their people by reviving and reintroducing their Hebrew mother tongue! O my friends of the Occident:

the mother tongue is and will always be the mistress in the house of nationhood, the world language must and will always be but the obedient and useful maidservant of her superior mistress.

Alláh'u'Abhá! *With this Bahá'í greeting the Master withdraws.*[127]

⤺

We drove for nearly two hours. It was raining most of the time, but the country was beginning to be quite verdant. 'Abdu'l-Bahá taught me a few words of Persian, and I taught Him a few of Esperanto! (Dr John Ebenezer Esslemont)[128]

⤺

In addition to this, he [Shoghi Effendi] devoted much attention, during the early years of his Guardianship, when Esperanto was rapidly spreading, particularly in Europe, to encouraging the publication of the Bahá'í Esperanto Gazette, explaining to its editor that his interest was due to 'my great desire to promote in such parts of the Bahá'í world as present circumstances permit the study of an international language'. (From Rabbání, *Priceless Pearl*)[129]

⤺

In addition to these personal relationships Shoghi Effendi had far more contact with certain non-Bahá'í organizations than is commonly supposed. This was particularly true of the Esperantists, whose whole object was to bring about the fulfilment of the Bahá'í principle that a universal auxiliary language must be adopted in the interests of World Peace. We have copies of his personal messages to the Universal Congress of Esperantists held in 1927, 1928, 1929, 1930 and 1931, and he no doubt sent many messages of a similar nature at other times. Shoghi Effendi not only responded warmly when there was any overture made to him, but often took the initiative himself in sending Bahá'í representatives, chosen by him, to various conferences whose interests coincided with those of the Bahá'ís. We thus find him writing to the Universal Esperantist Association, in 1927, that Martha Root and Julia Goldman will attend their Danzig Congress as official Bahá'í representatives, and that he trusts this 'will serve to strengthen the ties of fellowship that bind the Esperantists and the followers of Bahá'u'lláh, one of whose cardinal principles . . . is the adoption of an international auxiliary language for all humanity.' In his letter addressed to the delegates and friends attending this nineteenth Universal Congress of Esperantists he writes:

My dear fellow workers in the service of humanity,
   I take great pleasure in addressing you and wishing you . . . from all my heart the fullest success in the work you are doing for the promotion of the good of humanity.
   It will interest you, I am sure, to learn that as the result of the repeated and emphatic admonitions of 'Abdu'l-Bahá His many followers even in the most dis- tant villages and hamlets of Persia, where the light of Western civilization has hardly penetrated as yet, as well as in other lands throughout the East, are strenu- ously and enthusiastically engaged in the study and

teaching of Esperanto, for whose future they cherish the highest hopes . . . (From Rabbání, *Priceless Pearl*)[130]

∽

The Bahá'ís should adopt Esperanto at present as a universal language, even if only a temporary one. (Attributed to Shoghi Effendi)[131]

∽

Appendix
Writings about Other Languages¹³²

Writings of Bahá'u'lláh

Thou hast written concerning languages. Both Arabic and Persian are laudable. That which is desired of a language is that it convey the intent of the speaker, and either language can serve this purpose. And since in this day the Orb of divine knowledge hath risen in the firmament of Persia, that tongue deserveth every praise. (Tablet to Mánikchí Ṣáḥib: *Lawḥ-i-Mánikchí Ṣáḥib*)¹³³

His last question: 'Most of the Tablets that we have seen are in Arabic. However, since the Beloved in this age is of Persian descent, the Arabic tongue should be abandoned and discarded. For to this day the Arabs themselves have not understood the meaning of the Qur'án, whereas the Persian language is highly prized, lauded and admired among the dwellers of the inhabited quarter of the globe. And just as the Persian of the present day is superior to Arabic, so too is Old Persian, which is greatly favoured by the people of India and others. It would therefore be preferable if the words of God, magnified be His mention, were hereafter mainly delivered in pure Persian, since it attracteth the hearts to a greater degree. It is moreover requested that the reply to these questions be graciously written in pure Persian.'

The Persian tongue is in truth exceedingly sweet and pleasing, and ever since this request was submitted in His most blessed and exalted court, numerous Tablets have been revealed in that language. As to the statement concerning the Qur'án implying that its outward meaning hath not been understood, in reality it hath been interpreted in numerous ways and translated into countless languages. That which men have been unable to grasp are its hidden mysteries and inner meanings. And all that they have said or will say is limited in scope and should be seen as commensurate with their rank and station. For none can fathom its true meaning save God, the One, the Incomparable, the AllKnowing. . . .

The distinguished Ṣáḥib hath written: 'Since the Beloved in this age is of Persian descent, the Arabic tongue should be abandoned and discarded.' In this connection these sublime words issued from the Pen of the Most High, magnified and exalted be His glory: 'Both Arabic and Persian are laudable. That which is desired of a language is that it convey the intent of the speaker, and either language can serve this purpose. And since in this day the Orb of knowledge hath risen in the firmament of Persia, this tongue deserveth every praise.'

The light of truth is indeed shining resplendent above the horizon of divine utterance, and hence no further elaboration is required from this evanescent soul or from others like unto him. Although there can be no question or doubt as to the sweetness of the Persian tongue, yet it hath not the scope of the Arabic. There are many things which have not been expressed in Persian, that is to say, words referring to such things have not been devised, whilst in Arabic there are several words describing the same thing. Indeed there existeth no language in the world as vast and comprehensive as Arabic. This statement is prompted by truth and fairness; otherwise it is clear that in this day the world is being illumined by the splendours of that Sun which hath dawned above the horizon of Persia, and that the merits of this sweet language can scarcely be overestimated. (Responses to questions of Mánikchí Ṣáḥib from a Tablet to Mírzá Abu'l-Faḍl)[134]

WRITINGS OF 'ABDU'L-BAHÁ

O maid-servant of God! Study Persian and acquire it more day by day, for by the study of this language great and boundless results are obtained. (Letter to an individual)[135]

ﺳ

Praise be to God! This is the dawn of the light of unity between the Eastern and Western people. In Persia the English language is being studied widely and in America the Persian tongue is beloved by some dear souls. In both countries the respective languages are being studied. This is in itself a proof that the East and the West (literally, place of sunrise and sunset) shall clasp hands as two families. The standard of unity shall be raised, and the means of love and friendship will be accomplished.

Endeavour to complete the study of the Persian – thus mayest thou read the Tablets of the Blessed Beauty and mayest translate them, and without the interpreter's aid thou mayest read all my letters to thee. (Letter to an individual)[136]

LETTERS WRITTEN ON BEHALF OF SHOGHI EFFENDI

Shoghi Effendi was very glad to hear that you are planning to study Persian very seriously. Should you do it you will obtain ample reward for your labours, for you will then be able to go straight to the writings themselves. (Letter of 14 January 1932)[137]

◦~

Shoghi Effendi was very glad to know that the new edition of the Íqán has reached you safely and that you are going to use it in going over your translation into German. He is surely very sorry that not knowing Persian you cannot go to the very original. He sincerely hopes that before long we will have some of the younger members of the German Bahá'ís who would make translation their life-work, and with that object in mind make a thorough study of Persian and Arabic. They would surely be rendering a wonderful service to their nation as well as to the Faith as a whole. (Letter of 24 February 1932)[138]

◦~

To study Persian is excellent, and next to this make every effort to master the English language, as it will enable you to speak to people of all races and to read the wide literature on the Faith and allied subjects which is available in that tongue. (Letter of 1 August 1941)[139]

◦~

You are quite free of course to study Persian or Arabic if you wish to; but he would advise you to concentrate on English, as all the important teachings of the Faith have been translated into English and are authoritative. To grasp in the original Persian and Arabic the Teachings would be an infinitely more difficult task and require a great deal more time, particularly as you are so far away from the countries in which these languages are spoken. (Letter of 3 May 1956)[140]

TEXTS WRITTEN ON BEHALF OF THE UNIVERSAL HOUSE OF JUSTICE

While the Research Department has, to date, not been able to locate any statements in the Bahá'í Writings concerning the Persian language within the context of a discussion of the universal language, there are a number of passages in which the believers in the West were encouraged by 'Abdu'l-Bahá and Shoghi Effendi to study Persian . . .

Since the Writings of the Faith were, from the earliest days, translated into English, 'Abdu'l-Bahá and Shoghi Effendi encouraged the believers in Europe and Asia to study English. There is, however, nothing in the Bahá'í teachings to suggest that English will be the international auxiliary language. (Memorandum of the Research Department, 1995)[141]

GLOSSARY

'Abdu'l-Bahá (1844–1921)
In His will and testament, Bahá'u'lláh conferred the stewardship of the Bahá'í community and the interpretation of the Bahá'í sacred writings to His eldest son, 'Abbás Effendi, known by the title 'Abdu'l-Bahá (Servant of Bahá).

the Báb (1819–50)
Founder of the Bábí religion, which preceded the Bahá'í Faith. In 1844, at the age of 24, Siyyid 'Alí-Muḥammad, a merchant from Shiraz, Iran, claimed to be the Qá'im (or Mahdi), as promised in Shí'á Islam. His writings, along with those of Bahá'u'lláh, constitute the core scriptures of the Bahá'í Faith. Siyyid 'Alí-Muḥammad assumed the title of the Báb, meaning 'Gate'.

Bahá'í Esperanto League (BEL)
The official organization of Bahá'í Esperantists. It was founded on 19 March 1973 with the approval of the Universal House of Justice. As of 2011, BEL had 400 members in 64 countries. Recent BEL activities include participation in the Esperanto World Congresses, occasional publication of Bahá'í articles in Esperanto magazines and the translation of Bahá'í documents.

Bahá'í International Community (BIC)

A non-governmental organization (NGO), with offices in New York, Geneva, Brussels, Addis Ababa and Jakarta that represents the Bahá'ís worldwide at the United Nations (UN), the European Union (EU) and other global institutions. BIC collaborates consultatively with the UN and its agencies, with states, inter-governmental organizations and NGOs in such areas as gender equality, human rights and the environment.

Bahá'u'lláh, Baha'o'llah (1817–92)

The founder of the Bahá'í Faith (1863), born Mírzá Ḥusayn-'Alí in 1817 to a noble family in the Persian province of Mázandarán. Initially a leader in the Bábí movement, Bahá'u'lláh (the Glory of God) wrote over a hundred of the principal Bahá'í scriptures throughout 40 years of exile and imprisonment – most importantly the Kitáb-i-Aqdas (Book of Laws) and the Kitáb-i-Íqán (Book of Certitude).

Cart, Théophile (1855–1931)

French linguist who was one of the leading personalities of the Esperanto movement during the first three decades of the 20th century.

Epistle to the Son of the Wolf (Lawḥ-i-Ibn-i-Dhib)

The final major work of Bahá'u'lláh. It was written to an Islamic cleric who, along with his ecclesiastic father, violently opposed and persecuted Bahá'ís.

Guardian of the Faith

See Shoghi Effendi

Kitáb-i-Aqdas (Book of Laws)
'The Most Holy Book' revealed by Bahá'u'lláh as the framework for society in the Bahá'í era.

Kitáb-i-Íqán (Book of Certitude)
An exposition of essential teachings on the nature of God and religion revealed by Bahá'u'lláh.

the Master
See 'Abdu'l-Bahá.

pilgrims' notes
Unofficial records by individuals of their meetings with the central figures of the Bahá'í Faith. Though widely circulated, these notes cannot be confirmed as accurate representations of what, for instance, 'Abdu'l-Bahá or Shoghi Effendi may have said. Authors may have incorrectly heard, written, remembered, translated, quoted and/or understood remarks made.

Rúḥíyyih Rabbání (1910–2000)
Wife of Shoghi Effendi. Born Mary Sutherland Maxwell in 1910 in New York, she was the only child of William Sutherland Maxwell and his wife May Bolles.

Shoghi Effendi, Shoghi Effendi Rabbání (1897–1957)
Great-grandson of Bahá'u'lláh; appointed Guardian of the Faith by his grandfather 'Abdu'l-Bahá. By the time of his death, Shoghi Effendi had overseen the building of the Bahá'í world community from the local level up, such that by 1963 the Universal House of Justice could be elected.

Spiritual Assemblies

In the Bahá'í Faith, administrative authority resides not with individuals or clergy but with bodies of nine members annually elected at the local and national levels, respectively referred to as 'Local Spiritual Assemblies' (LSAs) and 'National Spiritual Assemblies' (NSAs).

Tablets

Letters, treatises and other topical, self-contained texts that were written either in the hand of the central figures of the Bábí and Bahá'í Faiths or by their amanuenses.

the Universal House of Justice

The international Bahá'í governing body, composed of nine members, which has its seat in Haifa, Israel. Every five years since 1963, representatives of the world's NSAs elect members of this institution, which exercises supreme legislative authority and guidance over the affairs of the Bahá'í world community.

Zamenhof, Ludwig Lazarus (1859–1917)

A Polish eye doctor and the originator of Esperanto ('one who hopes'), the most widespread artificial or constructed language to date, named after the above pseudonym.

Bibliography

Note: Unpublished letters listed in the Bibliography are housed at the Bahá'í International Archives, Haifa, Israel.

'Abdu'l-Bahá. 'On the Importance of Divine Civilization', translated from the Persian by Mirza Ahmad Sohrab. *Asiatic Quarterly Review*, vol. 1, no. 2 (April 1913).

— Letter to Dr Ameen Fareed (Amin Farid), in *The British Esperantist*, vol. 7, no. 84 (Dec. 1911).

— *Paris Talks*. London: Bahá'í Publishing Trust, 1995.

— *The Promulgation of Universal Peace*. Wilmette, IL: Bahá'í Publishing Trust, 1982.

— *Selections from the Writings of 'Abdu'l-Bahá*. Haifa: Bahá'í World Centre, 1978.

— *Tablets of Abdul-Baha Abbas*. New York: Bahá'í Publishing Committee; vol. 1, 1930; vol. 2, 1940; vol. 3, 1930.

Abdul Baha on Divine Philosophy. Compiled by Isabel Fraser Chamberlain. Boston: The Tudor Press, 1918.

'Abdu'l-Bahá in London. London: Bahá'í Publishing Trust, 1987.

'Aus dem Schatz der Erinnerungen an Abbas Effendi, 'Abdu'l-Bahá. Haifa: Zweiter Brief von Frau Dr. med. J. Fallscheer an Frau A. Schwarz', in *Sonne der Wahrheit*, bd. 10, heft 4. Stuttgart: 1930. ['From the Wealth of Memories of Abbas Effendi, 'Abdu'l-Bahá: Second letter from Mrs. J. Fallscheer MD, to Mrs. A. Schwarz', in *Sonne der Wahrheit* (*The Sun of Truth*), vol. 10, no. Stuttgart, 1930). Provisional translation by the editors from the German.

Bahá'í International Community. *Rights of Minorities: Comments on the Draft Declaration. Statement Submitted to the 48th Session of the United Nations Commission on Human Rights*. BIC Doc. no 92-0207. Geneva: Bahá'í International Community, 1992.

87

— *Turning Point for All Nations: A Statement of the Bahá'í International Community on the Occasion of the 50th Anniversary of the United Nations*. New York: Bahá'í International Community United Nations Office, 1995.

Bahai Scriptures. New York: Brentano's, 1923.

The Bahá'í World. vols. 1–12 (1925–54). rpt. Wilmette, IL: Bahá'í Publishing Trust, 1980.

Bahá'í World Faith. Wilmette, IL: Bahá'í Publishing Trust, 2nd ed. 1976.

Bahá'u'lláh. *Epistle to the Son of the Wolf*. Wilmette, IL: Bahá'í Publishing Trust, 1988.

— Glad-Tidings: *Bishárát*, in *Tablets of Bahá'u'lláh*, pp. 19–29.

— *Gleanings from the Writings of Bahá'u'lláh*. Wilmette, IL: Bahá'í Publishing Trust, 1983.

— *The Kitáb-i-Aqdas*. Haifa: Bahá'í World Centre, 1992.

— *Nafahát-i-Quds*. New Delhi: Bahá'í Publishing Trust, n.d.

— 'Responses to questions of Mánikchí Ṣáḥib from a Tablet to Mírzá Abu'l-Faḍl', in *Tabernacle of Unity*, pp. 13–54.

— Splendours: *Ishráqát*, in *Tablets of Bahá'u'lláh*, pp. 99–134.

— *Tabernacle of Unity*. Haifa: Bahá'í World Centre, 2006.

— Tablet to Mánikchí Ṣáḥib: *Lawh-i-Mánikchí Ṣáḥib*, in *Tabernacle of Unity*, pp. 1–11.

— Tablet of Maqṣúd: *Lawh-i-Maqṣúd*, in *Tablets of Bahá'u'lláh*, pp. 159–78.

— Tablet of the World: *Lawh-i-Dunyá*, in *Tablets of Bahá'u'lláh*, pp. 81–97.

— *Tablets of Bahá'u'lláh revealed after the Kitáb-i-Aqdas*. Haifa: Bahá'í World Centre, 1978.

— Words of Paradise: *Kalimát-i-Firdawsíyyih*, in *Tablets of Bahá'u'lláh*, pp. 55–80.

Bolles, Jeanne. 'The Bahai Movement and Esperanto', in *Star of the West*, vol. 11, no. 17, 19 January 1921, pp. 286–7, 290–1.

The British Esperantist (Journal of British Esperanto Association), vol. 7, no. 84 (December 1911); February 1913.

Cart, Théophile. 'Vizito al Abdul Baha', *Lingvo Internacia*, March 1913.

— *Vortoj de Profesoro Cart.* Jaslo, Poland: Esperantista Voco, 1927.

Century of Light. Haifa: Bahá'í World Centre, 2001.

Couturat, Louis. *A Plea for an International Language.* London: George Henderson, 1903.

— and L. Leau. *Histoire de la Langue Universelle.* Paris: Hachette, 1903.

Crystal, David. *English as a Global Language.* Cambridge: Cambridge University Press, 1997.

Dalgarno, George. *Ars Signorum: Vulgo Character Universaliset Lingua Philosophica.* London: J. Hayes, 1661.

Eco, Umberto. *The Search for the Perfect Language.* Oxford: Basil Blackwell, 1995.

Esslemont, John E. *Bahá'u'lláh and the New Era.* Wilmette, IL: Bahá'í Publishing Trust, 1980.

Gollmer, Werner. *Mein Herz ist bei euch: 'Abdu'l-Bahá in Deutschland.* Hofheim-Langenhain: Bahá'í-Verlag, 1988.

Heller, Wendy. *Lidia.* Oxford: George Ronald, 1985.

Holy Bible. King James Version. London: Collins, 1839.

Jespersen, Otto. *Selected Writings of Otto Jespersen.* London: George Allen & Unwin, 1962.

Knowlson, James S. *Universal Language Schemes in England and France, 1600–1800.* Toronto: University of Toronto Press, 1975.

Lenneberg, E. H. *The Biological Foundations of Language.* New York: John Wiley, 1967.

Lights of Guidance: A Bahá'í Reference File. Compiled by Helen Hornby. New Delhi: Bahá'í Publishing Trust, 5th ed. 1997.

Lingvo Internacia, March 1913.

Maḥmúd-i-Zarqání. *Maḥmúd's Diary.* Oxford: George Ronald, 1998.

Maxwell, May and Mary (Rúḥíyyih Khánum). *Haifa Notes of Shoghi Effendi's Word,* vol. 2. Unpublished notes, 1937.

Meyjes, Gregory Paul P. *The Choice of an Auxiliary Language for the World: Perspectives within the Context of Contemporary Linguistics*. Unpublished MA dissertation. Lancaster, UK: University of Lancaster, 1984.

— 'Language and universalization: A "linguistic ecology" reading of Bahá'í writ'. *The Journal of Bahá'í Studies*, vol. 9, no. 1 (1999), pp. 51–63.

— 'Language and world order in Bahá'í perspective: A new paradigm revealed', in T. Omoniyi and J. A. Fishman (eds.). *Explorations in the Sociology of Language and Religion*, pp. 26–41. Amsterdam: John Benjamins, 2006.

Momen, Moojan. *Dr. John Ebenezer Esslemont*. London: Bahá'í Publishing Trust, 1975.

La Nova Tago, The Bahá'í International Esperanto Gazette. Weinheim, Germany, 1920s–1930s.

Pei, Mario. *One Language for the World*. New York: Devin-Adair, 1961.

The Principle of an International Auxiliary Language. A compilation made by the Bahá'í World Centre on behalf of the Universal House of Justice. Haifa: 1985.

Rabbání, Rúḥíyyih. *The Guardian of the Bahá'í Faith*. London: Bahá'í Publishing Trust, 1988.

— *The Priceless Pearl*. London: Bahá'í Publishing Trust, 1969.

Rosenfelder, Mark. *The Language Construction Kit*. Chicago: Yonagu Books, 2010.

Sapir, Edward. 'The function of an international auxiliary language', in D.G. Mandelbaum (ed.), *Selected Writings of Edward Sapir*, pp. 110–21. Berkeley: University of California Press, 1949.

Schleyer, Johann M. *Grammatik der Universalsprache für alle Erdbewohner, Volapük*. Konstanz: Verl. von Schleyer's Weltspràche-Zentràlbüro, 1885.

Shoghi Effendi. *God Passes By*. Wilmette, IL: Bahá'í Publishing Trust, rev. ed. 1995.

— *High Endeavors: Messages to Alaska*. [Anchorage]: National Spiritual Assembly of the Bahá'ís of Alaska, 1976.

— Letters

18 October 1925 to an individual, translated from the Persian.

30 January 1926 to an individual, translated from the Persian.

18 May 1927 to an individual, translated from the Persian.

4 May 1928 to the Esperanto Congress in Antwerp.

18 May 1928 on behalf of Shoghi Effendi to an individual.

30 August 1928 to an individual.

19 September 1930 on behalf of Shoghi Effendi to an individual.

14 January 1932 on behalf of Shoghi Effendi to an individual.

24 February 1932 on behalf of Shoghi Effendi to Dr Mühlschlegel.

14 March 1932 on behalf of Shoghi Effendi to George Winthrop Lee.

30 August 1933 on behalf of Shoghi Effendi to two individuals.

17 April 1936 on behalf of Shoghi Effendi to an individual.

5 May 1936 on behalf of Shoghi Effendi to an individual.

26 December 1936 on behalf of Shoghi Effendi to an individual.

28 May 1937 on behalf of Shoghi Effendi to an individual.

4 June 1937 on behalf of Shoghi Effendi to a National Spiritual Assembly.

9 August 1937 on behalf of Shoghi Effendi to an individual.

31 October 1937 on behalf of Shoghi Effendi to George Winthrop Lee.

24 April 1939 on behalf of Shoghi Effendi to an individual.

1 August 1941 on behalf of Shoghi Effendi to the daughters of N. R. Vakil.

25 January 1943 on behalf of Shoghi Effendi to an individual.

30 June 1944 on behalf of Shoghi Effendi to an individual.

17 October 1944 on behalf of Shoghi Effendi to an individual.

    5 April 1947 on behalf of Shoghi Effendi to an individual.
    31 March 1948 on behalf of Shoghi Effendi to an individual.
    25 March 1949 on behalf of Shoghi Effendi to an individual.
    3 May 1956 on behalf of Shoghi Effendi to the Bahá'ís of Malmö, Sweden.

— *The Light of Divine Guidance: The Messages from the Guardian of the Bahá'í Faith to the Bahá'ís of Germany and Austria.* 2 vols. Hofheim-Langenhain: Bahá'í-Verlag, 1982/1985.

— *Messages of Shoghi Effendi to the Indian Subcontinent, 1923–1957.* New Delhi: Bahá'í Publishing Trust, 1995.

— *The World Order of Bahá'u'lláh.* Wilmette, IL: Bahá'í Publishing Trust, 1991.

Sonne der Wahrheit: Zeitschrift für Weltreligion und Welteinheit. Stuttgart: National Spiritual Assembly of the Bahá'ís of Germany and Austria, vol. 18, 1 Dec. 1921, 1947.

Star of the West. rpt. Oxford: George Ronald, 1984.

The Universal House of Justice. Letters by and on behalf of,
    8 June 1971 to an individual.
    20 July 1972 to an individual.
    May 1974 to the Secretary of Bahaa Esperanto-Ligo.
    29 December 1974 to a National Spiritual Assembly.
    2 March 1976 to a National Spiritual Assembly.
    6 October 1976 to the Bahaa Esperanto-Ligo.
    6 July 1977 to an individual.
    8 June 1980 to an individual.
    2 June 1982 to an individual.
    26 March 1986 to an individual.
    17 June 1986 to an individual.
    17 September 1986 to National Spiritual Assemblies in Europe.
    30 June 1987 to the president of Universala Esperanto-Asocio.
    2 August 1990 to an individual.
    21 December 1990 to an individual.
    5 September 1991 to an individual.
    12 January 1994 to an individual.

11 November 1996 to an individual.

— Memoranda of the Research Department of the Universal House of Justice

16 August 1995 to an individual.

17 March 1996 to a former editor of the present volume.

4 June 1997 to the Bahá'í Esperanto League.

— *The Promise of World Peace.* Haifa: Bahá'í World Centre, 1985.

Wilkins, John. *An Essay Towards a Real Character and a Philosophical Language.* London: Gellibrant and Martin, 1668.

Zamenhof, Ludwig L. *An Attempt Towards an International Language.* New York: Holt, 1889.

.

FURTHER READING

Blanke, Detlev. *Internationale Plansprachen*. Berlin: Akademie-Verlag, 1985.

Bolton, Marjorie. *Zamenhof: Creator of Esperanto*. London: Routledge & Kegan Paul, 1960.

Burney, P. *Les Langues Internationales*. Paris: Presses Universitaires de France, 1962.

Cram, David and Jaap Maat (eds.). *George Dalgarno on Universal Language: The Art of Signs (1661), The Deaf and Dumb Man's Tutor (1680), and the Unpublished Papers*. Oxford: Oxford University Press, 2001.

Clark, Walter J. *International Language, Past, Present & Future: With Specimens of Esperanto and Grammar* (1907). Rpt. London: Forgotten Books, 2013.

Fettes, Mark, and Suzanne Bolduc (eds.). *Al lingva demokratio/ Towards Linguistic Democracy/Vers la démocratie linguistique*. Rotterdam: Universala Esperanto-Asocio, 1998.

Forster, Peter G. *The Esperanto Movement*. The Hague: Mouton, 1982.

Guérard, Albert L. *A Short History of the International Language Movement* (1922). Rpt. London: Forgotten Books, 2013.

Houghton, Stephen C. *The Master Language: An Outline of the Principles and Rules of a Proposed International Auxiliary Language*. Charleston: Nabu Press, 2012.

Jespersen, Otto. *An International Language*. London: Routledge, 2006.

Large, Andrew. *The Artificial Language Movement*. Oxford: Basil Blackwell, 1985.

Meyjes, Gregory Paul P. 'Language and universalization: a "linguistic ecology" reading of Bahá'í writ'. *The Journal of Bahá'í Studies*, vol. 9, no. 1 (1999), pp. 51–63.

— 'Language and world order in Bahá'í perspective: a new paradigm revealed', in T. Omoniyi and J. A. Fishman (eds.). *Explorations in the Sociology of Language and Religion*, pp. 26–41. Amsterdam: John Benjamins, 2006.

Ogden, C.K. *Basic English Versus the Artificial Languages*. London: Kegan Paul, 1935.

Slaughter, Mary M. *Universal Languages and Scientific Taxonomy in the Seventeenth Century*. Cambridge: Cambridge University Press, 1982.

Tonkin, Humphrey (ed.). *Esperanto, Interlinguistics, and Planned Language*. Lanham: University Press of America, 1997.

Tonkin, Humphrey. *Esperanto and International Language Problems: A Research Bibliography*. Washington DC: Esperantic Studies Association, 1977.

Universal Declaration of Linguistic Rights. Barcelona, Romanyà Valls: 6 June 1996.

Notes and References

1. Bahá'u'lláh, *Kitáb-i-Aqdas*, para. 189.
2. Bahá'u'lláh, *Gleanings*, pp. 249–50.
3. ibid. p. 215.
4. Shoghi Effendi, *World Order*, p. 42.
5. See, for example, Bahá'í International Community, *Rights of Minorities*.
6. Bahá'u'lláh, *Kitáb-i-Aqdas*, para. 189.
7. Bahá'u'lláh, *Epistle*, pp. 28–9.
8. In Bahá'u'lláh, *Kitáb-i-Aqdas*, note 193.
9. Attributed to 'Abdu'l-Bahá, in *Abdul Baha on Divine Philosophy*, p. 84.
10. e.g. Eco, *Search for the Perfect Language*.
11. Questioning the applicability of 'globalization', Meyjes proposes the term 'universalization' (Meyjes, 'Language and universalization') in this context.
12. Knowlson, *Universal Language Schemes*.
13. And out of the ground the LORD God formed every beast of the field, and every fowl of the air; and brought them unto Adam to see what he would call them: and whatsoever Adam called every living creature, that was the name thereof' (Gen. 2:19, KJV).
14. Bahá'u'lláh, *Tablets*, p. 68.
15. Couturat, *Plea for an International Language*.
16. Jespersen, *Selected Writings*.
17. Sapir, 'The function of an international auxiliary language'.
18. Schleyer, *Grammatik der Universalsprache für alle Erdbewohner*.
19. Pei, *One Language for the World*.
20. Zamenhof, *Attempt Towards an International Language*.
21. Attributed to 'Abdu'l-Bahá, in *'Abdu'l-Bahá in London*, p. 94.
22. Heller, *Lidia*.

97

23. Attributed to 'Abdu'l-Bahá, in *'Abdu'l-Bahá in London*, p. 94.

24. For a more elaborate discussion of the following issues in Bahá'í perspective, see Meyjes, 'Language and world order in Bahá'í perspective'.

25. See Rosenfelder, *Language Construction Kit*.

26. Meyjes, *Choice of an Auxiliary Language for the World*.

27. Lenneberg, *Biological Foundations of Language*.

28. Attributed to 'Abdu'l-Bahá, in *Abdul Baha on Divine Philosophy*, p. 84.

29. Crystal, *English as a Global Language*.

30. Shoghi Effendi, *World Order*, p. 193.

31. Bahá'u'lláh, *Kitáb-i-Aqdas*, para. 189.

32. ibid. See also second passage, section V (Texts by and on behalf of the Universal House of Justice).

33. Bahá'u'lláh, 'Bishárát', *Tablets*, p. 22.

34. Bahá'u'lláh, 'Kalimát-i-Firdawsíyyih', *Tablets*, p. 68.

35. Bahá'u'lláh, 'Lawḥ-i-Dunyá', *Tablets*, p. 89.

36. Bahá'u'lláh, 'Ishráqát', *Tablets*, p. 127.

37. Bahá'u'lláh, 'Lawḥ-i-Maqṣúd', *Tablets*, pp. 165–6.

38. ibid. p. 166.

39. Bahá'u'lláh, *Epistle*, pp. 137–9.

40. Bahá'u'lláh, 'Nafaḥát-i-Quds', pp. 5–8. Provisional translation of the original Arabic Tablet, including a quotation from Qur'án 20:107, approved by the Universal House of Justice for inclusion in this book.

41. Letter to Mrs Jane Elizabeth Whyte, in 'Abdu'l-Bahá, *Selections*, pp. 31–2. Mrs Jane Elizabeth Whyte, of Charlotte Square, Edinburgh, was the wife of Reverend Alexander Whyte, Moderator of the General Assembly of the Free Church of Scotland. In 1906 Mrs Whyte visited 'Abdu'l-Bahá in 'Akká and in 1913 'Abdu'l-Bahá stayed with the Whytes during His visit to Scotland.

42. 'Abdu'l-Bahá, *Selections*, p. 301. Excerpted from a reply to a letter addressed to 'Abdu'l-Bahá by the Committee at The Hague. The Tablet, dated 17 December 1919, is described by Shoghi Effendi in *God Passes By* as being of 'far-reach-

ing importance'. (p. 308)

43. 'Abdu'l-Bahá, *Selections,* p. 308.

44. 'Abdu'l-Bahá, *Tablets*, vol. 2, p. 596.

45. ibid. p. 692.

46. 'Abdu'l-Bahá, quoted in *Star of the West*, vol. 11, no. 1, pp. 10–11. A slightly different translation is also found in 'On the Importance of Divine Civilization', translated from the Persian original by Mirza Ahmad Sohrab in the *Asiatic Quarterly Review*, vol. 1, no. 2 (April 1913).

47. 'Abdu'l-Bahá, *Tablets*, n.p. Revised and authorized translation from the Persian provided to the editors in 1996 by the Research Department of the Universal House of Justice.

48. Tablet of 'Abdu'l-Bahá to the Honorable William Sulzer (ex-governor of New York), 18 June 1919, in *Star of the West*, vol. 10, no. 17, p. 315.

49. Letter to Dr Ameen Fareed (Amín Faríd), based on the original as published in *The British Esperantist*, vol. 7, no. 84 (December 1911). This edited provisional version has been made by reference to the Persian original.

50. Excerpts in this section are based on handwritten notes taken by individuals listening to 'Abdu'l-Bahá's talks. As they are not based on authenticated written documents, their reliability and fidelity to 'Abdu'l-Bahá's words and/or intent cannot be conclusively established. They are nonetheless included for their detail and their pertinence.

51. Attributed to 'Abdu'l-Bahá in *Abdul Baha on Divine Philosophy*, p. 84.

52. A longer version of this talk appearing in 1921 includes these words at this point: 'This unification of languages had never crossed the minds of the thinkers of the past ages, and in reality it was an impossibility in those times, because there was no freedom in going and coming, and no travelling and no intercourse between the various countries. Now the means of communication and transport are greatly increased, therefore it is necessary and it is possible to bring about the use of this international language.' (*Star of the*

West, vol. 11, no. 18, 7 February 1921, p. 302)

53. The 1921 translation includes these words at this point: 'Let us hope for that day, when even the boundaries of native languages will be swept away and the world will enjoy one language. What greater bounty is there than this? What more munificent welfare is there than this? Then the world of humanity will become the delectable paradise, just as it is said that in heaven there is one language.' (ibid. p. 303)

54. The 1921 translation includes these words at this point: 'Take, for example, a family in which the various members speak each a different language; how difficult it is for them to convey their thoughts to one another, and how great and wonderful it is when they are able easily to understand one another's thoughts. For if they know one another's language, they will go on very rapidly; there is no doubt whatever about this.' (ibid. p. 306)

55. Address delivered in Edinburgh, 7 January 1913 under the auspices of the Edinburgh Esperanto Society. From *The British Esperantist*, February 1913. This was reprinted in English in *Star of the West*, vol. 4, no. 2 (9 April 1913), pp. 34–6; and with a different translation in English and in Esperanto in *Star of the West*, vol. 11, no. 18 (7 February 1921), pp. 299–303, 306. The opening two paragraphs were reproduced with slight differences in *Star of the West*, vol. 17, no. 6 (September 1926), p. 201 as a one-page quotation from 'Abdu'l-Bahá.

56. The talk is prefaced by this account of the setting:

> His Excellency ABDUL BAHA addressed the Paris Esperanto group on February 12, 1913, at the banquet which was accorded him at the Hotel Moderne in that city. M. Bourlet, President of the Paris Esperanto Society, in introducing Abdul Baha, said that one of the principles of the great world religion which he was promulgating, was the establishment of a universal language.
>
> There was a deep silence as Abdul Baha arose.

He spoke in Persian, M. Hippolyte Dreyfus of Paris interpreting into French. Here and there one noted that the French translation was undergoing still further interpretation by Esperantists for the benefit of neighbours who did not understand French but knew Esperanto, – the occasion itself offering a noteworthy argument for the imminent need of a universal tongue. (*Abdul Baha on Divine Philosophy*, p. 141)

57. This talk, with minor variations in translation, appears as chapter 4 of *Abdul Baha on Divine Philosophy* (1918), pp. 141–6 and in *Star of the West*, vol. 4, no. 2, 9 April 1913, pp. 36–7. Portions of it appear in *Star of the West*, vol. 17, no. 4, July 1926, p. 128; and in vol. 17, no. 5, August 1926, p. 160. A revised, abridged version appears in Esslemont, *Bahá'u'lláh and the New Era*, 5th revised ed. 1980, pp. 164–5. The following extended version was published in *Star of the West*, vol. 11, no. 17, 19 January 1921, pp. 287, 290–1.

In the human world there are two kinds of undertakings – universal and particular. The result of every universal undertaking is infinite, and the outcome of every particular undertaking is finite. In this age, all the human problems which create a general interest are universal and their results are likewise universal, for humanity has become interdependent. Today international laws have great influence, international politics are bringing nations nearer to one another. Therefore it is a general axiom that in the human world every universal affair commands attention, and its results and benefits are limitless; therefore let us say that every universal cause is divine and every special matter is human. For instance, the universal light is from the sun, therefore it is divine. Special light, which is electric and which has illumined this banquet hall is through the invention of man. By this I mean that all affairs in the world which are trying to establish solidarity between nations and infuse the spirit of universalism in the hearts are divine. Consequently we can say that the international auxiliary language is one of the greatest virtues of the world of humanity, for such an instrument will remove misunderstandings from amongst the people, and will cement their hearts together. The universal auxiliary language will be the means for each individual in the world of humanity to become enabled to be informed of the scientific accomplishments of all his fellow men.

The basis of knowledge and the excellencies of the world are to teach and be taught. To acquire sciences, and to teach them in turn, depends on language; therefore, when the international auxiliary language becomes universal, it is easily conceivable that the acquirement of knowledge and instruction will likewise become universal.

No doubt you are aware that in the past ages a common language shared by various nations created a spirit of interdependence and solidarity among them. For instance, one thousand three hundred years ago there were very many divergent nationalities in the Orient. There were Copts in Egypt, Syrians in Syria, Assyrians in Musel, Babylonians in Bagdad along the river Mesopotamia. There existed between these nations divergence of opinion and hatred, but as they were slowly brought near to one another, finding common interests, they made the Arabic a common vehicle of speech among them. The study of this common language by all made them as one nation. We know very well today that the Assyrians are not Arabs, that the Copts, Syrians, Chaldeans and Egyptians are not Arabs. Each one of these nations belongs to its own sphere of nationality, but, as they all began to study the Arabic language, making it a vehicle of intercommunication, today they are all considered as one. They are so united that it is impossible to break this indissoluble bond. Today in Syria there are many religious sects, such as Orthodox, Mussulman, the Dorzi, Nestorians and so on. As they all speak Arabic they are considered as one; if you ask any one of them he will say – I am an Arab, though in reality he is not. Some of them are Greeks, others are Jews, etc. In short, there are many different nations and religions in the Orient that are united through the benefit of a common language. In the world of existence an international auxiliary language is the greatest bond to unite the people. Today the causes of differences in Europe are the diversities of language. We say, this man is a German, the other is an Italian, then we meet an Englishman and then again a Frenchman. Although they belong to the same race, yet, language is the greatest barrier between them. Were a universal auxiliary language now in operation they would all be considered as one. Just as in the Orient a common language created common interests between the various nations, likewise, in this age, a universal auxiliary language would unite all the people of the world. The purpose of my remarks is, that, in the world of humanity, the greatest influence which will work for unity and harmony among the nations is the teaching of a universal language. Every intelligent man will bear testimony to this, and there is no further need for argument or evidence. Therefore His Holiness BAHA'O'LLAH wrote about this international language more than forty years ago. He says that as long as an international language is not invented complete union between the various sections of the world will be unrealized, for we observe that misunderstandings keep people from mutual association, and these misunderstandings will not be dispelled except through an international auxiliary language. Generally speaking the whole people of the Orient are not fully informed of the events in the West, neither can the Westerners put themselves in sympathetic touch with the Easterners – their thoughts are enclosed in a casket – the international language will be the master key to open it. Were we in possession of this universal language, the Western books could easily be translated into this language, and the Easterners be informed of their contents. In the same way the books of the East could be translated into that language for the benefit of the Westerners. Thus will the misunderstandings that exist between different religions be dispersed. They bring about warfare and strife, and it is impossible to remove them without this universal language being spread everywhere. I am an Easterner and on this account I know nothing of your thoughts because an international language is not yet in vogue. Likewise you of the West are shut out of my thoughts. If we had a common language both of us would be informed of the other's thoughts. Consequently the strongest means of universal progress towards the union of East and West is this language. It will make the whole world one home and will become the greatest impulse for human advancement. It will upraise the standard of the oneness of the world of humanity, it will make the earth one universal commonwealth. It will be the cause of love between the children of men. It will cause good fellowship between the various races. Now, praise be to God, that Dr. Zamenhof has invented the Esperanto language. It has all the potential qualities of becoming the international means of communication. All of us must be grateful and thankful to him for this noble effort, for in this way he has served his fellow-men well. He has invented a language which will bestow the greatest benefits on all people. With untiring effort and self sacrifice on the part of its devotees it will become universal. Therefore every one of us must study this language and spread it as far as possible so that day by day it may receive a broader recognition, be accepted by all nations and governments of the world and become a part of the curriculum in all the public schools. I hope that the language of all the future international conferences and congresses will become Esperanto, so that all people may acquire only two languages – one their own tongue and the other the international auxiliary language. Then perfect union will be established between all the people of the world. Consider how difficult it is today to communicate with various nations. If one studies fifty languages one may yet travel through a country and not know the language. I know several languages of the Orient, but do not know the Western tongues. If this international language were in force, having studied it, I should be able to speak it and you would have been directly informed of my thoughts, and a special friendship established between every one of us. The lack of such a language is now a great barrier.

Therefore I hope that you will make the utmost effort, so that this language of Esperanto may be widely spread. Send some teachers to Persia if you can, so that they may teach it to the young people, and I have written to Persia to tell some of the Persians to come here to study it.

I hope that this language will be promulgated very quickly and the world of humanity finds eternal peace; that all the nations may associate with one another and become as brothers and sisters, mothers and fathers; then each individual member of the body politic will be fully informed of the thoughts of all.

I am extremely grateful to you, and thank you for these lofty aims, for you have gathered at this banquet to further this language.

Your hope is to render a mighty service to the world of humanity, and for this great aim I congratulate you from the bottom of my heart.

58. 'Abdu'l-Bahá, *Paris Talks*, pp. 155–7.

59. A talk given in Stuttgart, Germany, 5 April 1913 at a gathering of Esperantists. Provisional translation made by the present editor, Dr Gregory Meyjes, from the German text, published in Gollmer, *Mein Herz ist bei euch: 'Abdu'l-Bahá in Deutschland*, pp. 62–6. The talk was also published in Esperanto in *La Nova Tago*, vol. 6, no. 2 (1930/31), pp. 17–20.

60. Attributed to 'Abdu'l-Bahá, in *'Abdu'l-Bahá in London*, p. 94.

61. A Message to Esperantists, given at the home of Mr and Mrs Arthur J. Parsons, Washington DC, 25 April 1912, in 'Abdu'l-Bahá, *Promulgation*, pp. 60–1.

62. From a talk at the Baptist Temple, Philadelphia, 9 June 1912, in ibid. p. 182.

63. From a talk at All Souls Unitarian Church, New York, 14 July 1912, in ibid. pp. 232–3.

64. From a talk at the Church of the Messiah, Montreal, 1 September 1912, in ibid. p. 300.

65. From a talk at St James Methodist Church, Montreal, 5 September 1912, in ibid. p. 318.

66. From a talk at the home of Juliet Thompson, New York, 15 November 1912, in ibid. pp. 434–5.

67. Answer to a question asked at the Golden Circle Club, Boston, 24 July 1912, in *Maḥmúd's Diary*, pp. 179–80.

68. From a talk given at the Unitarian Church, Montreal, 1 September 1912, in *Maḥmúd's Diary*, pp. 234–5. For another translation of 'Abdu'l-Bahá's talk see *Promulgation*, pp. 297–302.

69. Shoghi Effendi, *God Passes By*, p. 211.

70. ibid. p. 218.

71. Shoghi Effendi, *World Order*, p. 203.

72. From a letter of Shoghi Effendi to an individual, 18 October 1925, translated from the Persian.

73. From a letter written on behalf of Shoghi Effendi to an individual, 30 January 1926, translated from the Persian.

74. From a letter of Shoghi Effendi to the editor of *La Nova Tago*, in *Light of Divine Guidance*, vol. 1, pp. 25–6.

75. From a letter of Shoghi Effendi of 17 April 1927 addressed to the delegates and friends attending the Nineteenth Universal Congress of Esperanto, which took place in Danzig Free City from 28 July to 3 August 1927, in *Bahá'í World*, vol. 2, p. 269. The letter was read to one thousand delegates at the formal opening of the Congress.

76. From a letter written on behalf of Shoghi Effendi to an individual, 18 May 1927, translated from the Persian.

77. From a letter of Shoghi Effendi of 4 May 1928 to the delegates attending the Twentieth Universal Congress of Esperanto in Antwerp, Belgium, in *Bahá'í World*, vol. 3, pp. 347–8; and in *Star of the West*, vol. 19, no. 8 (November 1928), pp. 242–3. The Congress was held 3–11 August 1928 and was attended by 1,500 delegates from 42 countries. The letter was read at the opening session.

78. From a letter written on behalf of Shoghi Effendi to an individual, 18 May 1928.

79. From a letter of Shoghi Effendi to an individual, 30 August 1928. Emphases in the original.

80. From a letter written on behalf of Shoghi Effendi to an individual, 19 September 1930.

81. From a letter written on behalf of Shoghi Effendi to George Winthrop Lee, 14 March 1932. Mr Lee, of Brookline, Massachusetts, was secretary of the Esperanto Association of North America. He had been an Esperantist since 1906 and occasionally wrote to Shoghi Effendi suggesting that he learn Esperanto. See Heller, *Lidia*, pp. 178–9.

82. From a letter written on behalf of Shoghi Effendi to two individuals, 30 August 1933.

83. From a letter written on behalf of Shoghi Effendi, in *Light of Divine Guidance*, vol. 2, pp. 36–7. Emphasis in the original.

84. From a letter written on behalf of Shoghi Effendi to an individual, 17 April 1936.

85. From a letter written on behalf of Shoghi Effendi to an individual, 5 May 1936.

86. From a letter written on behalf of Shoghi Effendi to an individual, 26 December 1936.

87. From letter written on behalf of Shoghi Effendi to the National Spiritual Assembly of the United States and Canada, 4 June 1937, in *Lights of Guidance*, pp. 339–40.

88. From a letter written on behalf of Shoghi Effendi to an individual, 9 August 1937.

89. From a letter written on behalf of Shoghi Effendi to George Winthrop Lee, 31 October 1937. Emphases in the original. This extract also appears in Heller, *Lidia*, p. 179.

90. From a letter written on behalf of Shoghi Effendi to an individual, 24 April 1939.

91. From a letter written on behalf of Shoghi Effendi to an individual, 25 January 1943.

92. From a letter written on behalf of Shoghi Effendi to an individual, 30 June 1944.

93. From a letter written on behalf of Shoghi Effendi to an individual, 17 October 1944.

94. From a letter written on behalf of Shoghi Effendi to an individual, in *Light of Divine Guidance*, vol. 2, p. 53. Emphasis in original.

95. From a letter written on behalf of Shoghi Effendi to an individual, 5 April 1947.

96. From a letter written on behalf of Shoghi Effendi to an individual, 31 March 1948.

97. From a letter written on behalf of Shoghi Effendi to an individual, 25 March 1949.

98. Excerpt from a letter of the Universal House of Justice to the Peoples of World, October 1985, entitled *The Promise of World Peace*.

99. In Bahá'u'lláh, *Kitáb-i-Aqdas*, note 193.

100. Bahá'í International Community, *Turning Point for All Nations*, para. III, A.4.

101. *Century of Light*, p. 128.

102. From a letter by the Universal House of Justice to an individual, 8 June 1971.

103. From a letter written by the Universal House of Justice to an individual, 20 July 1972.

104. From a letter written on behalf of the Universal House of Justice to the Secretary of Bahaa Esperanto-Ligo, May 1974.

105. From a letter written on behalf of the Universal House of Justice to a National Spiritual Assembly, 29 December 1974.

106. From a letter written on behalf of the Universal House of Justice to a National Spiritual Assembly, 2 March 1976.

107. From a letter written on behalf of the Universal House of Justice to the Bahaa Esperanto-Ligo, 6 October 1976.

108. From a letter written on behalf of the Universal House of Justice to an individual, 6 July 1977.

109. From a letter written on behalf of the Universal House of Justice to an individual, 8 June 1980.

110. From a letter written on behalf of the Universal House of Justice to an individual, 2 June 1982.

111. 'Introduction', *The Principle of an International Auxiliary Language*, p. i, a compilation prepared in January 1985 at the instruction of the Universal House of Justice; the passage is also included in a Memorandum prepared by the Research Department at the instruction of the Universal House of Justice for an individual believer, 16 August 1995.

112. From a letter written on behalf of the Universal House of Justice to an individual, 26 March 1986.

113. From a letter written on behalf of the Universal House of Justice to an individual, 17 June 1986.

114. From a letter of the Universal House of Justice to National Spiritual Assemblies in Europe, 17 September 1986.

115. From a letter of the Universal House of Justice to the president of Universala Esperanto-Asocio, 30 June 1987.

116. From a letter written on behalf of the Universal House of Justice to an individual, 2 August 1990.

117. From a letter written on behalf of the Universal House of Justice to an individual, 21 December 1990.

118. From a letter written on behalf of the Universal House of Justice to an individual, 5 September 1991.

119. From a letter written on behalf of the Universal House of Justice to an individual, 12 January 1994.

120. From a letter written on behalf of the Universal House of Justice to an individual, 11 November 1996.

121. Memorandum prepared by the Research Department at the instruction of the Universal House of Justice for the Bahá'í Esperanto League, 4 June 1997.

122. The passages in this section come from a variety of sources, including informal handwritten notes, so-called 'pilgrims' notes', by various authors. Such sources are to be used with caution, especially when intended to represent words attributed to central figures of the Bahá'í Faith, for often their reliability or authenticity cannot be conclusively established. However relevant and of interest they may appear, they cannot be relied on as authoritative writings.

123. Attributed to 'Abdu'l-Bahá in *Bahai Scriptures*, p. 279. 'No original notes for this talk have been located and this utterance cannot be authenticated. The same extract also appears in a report of the address by Mr Joseph G. Hannen delivered at the Bahá'í Congress and Convention, held in Chicago, April 29 to May 2, 1916, and published in *Star of the West*, VII, no. 7 (July 13, 1916), p. 55. The extract is preceded by "At Clifton, England, 'Abdu'l-Bahá said . . .", with no date specified.' (Research Department of the Universal House of Justice, Memorandum to a previous editor, 1996) This passage is also published in Bolles, 'The Bahai Movement and Esperanto', p. 287.

124. Attributed to 'Abdu'l-Bahá in *Maḥmúd's Diary*, pp. 179–80. 'This exchange is also reported by Dr Zia Bagdadi in his article "'Abdu'l-Bahá in America", published in *Star of the West*, vol. 19, no. 10 (January 1929), p. 309: "The Syrians of Boston invited 'Abdu'l-Bahá to their club on July 24, 1912, and [were] anxious to know if the Arabic language would in time be the international language. 'Abdu'l-Bahá said: 'No!'" . . . It appears that the original source of this account is *Maḥmúd's Diary*.' (Research Department of the

Universal House of Justice, Memorandum to a previous
editor, 17 March 1996)

125. Paraphrase of an extract from the address of 'Abdu'l-Bahá
to the Theosophical Society of Paris, Thursday evening, 13
February 1913. 'It appears to us that the extract . . . actually
represents a paraphrase of an actual utterance of the
Master.' (Research Department of the Universal House of
Justice, Memorandum to a previous editor, 1996)

126. Cart, *Vortoj de Profesoro Cart*, pp. 118–20. An excerpt from
the article 'Vizito al Abdul Baha' by Prof. Théophile Cart
(1855–1931) in the Esperanto magazine *Lingvo Internacia*,
March 1913, and translated from Esperanto by John T.
Dale, Jr. It is also found in the collection of Cart's writings
published as *Vortoj de Profesoro Cart*.

   The passage is preceded by the following words:

   'On February 15, at four in the afternoon, one of my
   students from the School for Political Sciences, a
   Persian, had the kindness to lead me to 'Abdu'l-Bahá
   for a personal, intimate conversation.

      "Abdu'l-Bahá was old, but seemed not at all tired,
   at least during our conversation; he always spoke
   clearly, audibly, with very good humour, often laugh-
   ing when he told anecdotes.'

127. Attributed to 'Abdu'l-Bahá in 'Schatz der Erinnerungen',
n. p. On 20 January 1910, 'Abdu'l-Bahá answered questions
from two English women in the women's quarters of his
home in Haifa, Israel. Dr Fallscheer, the family physician,
was also present. A Persian friend from 'Akká translated
the words of the Master from Persian into English. Dr
Fallscheer's letter describing the encounter was published
20 years later.

128. Momen, *Esslemont*, p. 17.

129. Rabbání, *Priceless Pearl*, p. 207.

130. ibid. pp. 271–2; and Rabbání, *The Guardian*, pp. 124–5.

131. Attributed to Shoghi Effendi, in Maxwell, *Haifa Notes*, p.
36.

132. In Bahá'í perspective, realization of the IAL principle can occur through the use of any natural or constructed language. It does not presuppose a link between the selected IAL and a particular language, religion, technology, culture, history or such. The following excerpts from Bahá'í texts do not refer to the auxiliary language or to the principle of IAL. Instead, they address such matters as languages of Bahá'í revelation, the use of particular national languages, the translation of Bahá'í writings in specific areas of the world, etc. These passages refer to the merits of individual languages without reference to the IAL principle.

133. Bahá'u'lláh, 'Lawḥ-i-Mánikchí Ṣáḥib', *Tabernacle of Unity*, para. 1.7.

134. Bahá'u'lláh, 'Responses to questions of Mánikchí Ṣáḥib from a Tablet to Mírzá Abu'l-Faḍl', *Tabernacle of Unity*, paras. 2.54–8.

135. 'Abdu'l-Bahá, *Tablets*, vol. 2, p. 307.

136. ibid. p. 426.

137. From a letter written on behalf of Shoghi Effendi to an individual, 14 January 1932, in Shoghi Effendi, *Light of Divine Guidance*, vol. 2, p. 21.

138. From a letter written on behalf of Shoghi Effendi to Dr Mühlschlegel, 24 February 1932, in ibid. vol. 1, p. 40.

139. From a letter written on behalf of Shoghi Effendi to the daughters of N. R. Vakil, 1 August 1941, in *Messages of Shoghi Effendi to the Indian Subcontinent*, p. 205.

140. From a letter written on behalf of Shoghi Effendi to the Bahá'ís of Malmö, Sweden, 3 May 1956.

141. Memorandum prepared by the Research Department at the instruction of the Universal House of Justice for an individual, 16 August 1995.

Index

www.ingramcontent.com/pod-product-compliance
Lightning Source LLC
Chambersburg PA
CBHW050759250626
47155CB00005B/2136